BORN *from* ABOVE

An Exposition of John Chapter 3

Pastor Bill Randles

BORN FROM ABOVE: an exposition of John Chapter 3

Published by:
Believers in Grace Ministries
8585 C Avenue
Marion, Iowa 52302

ISBN: 978-096466-269-8

For more information about the author or his ministry, contact Billlrandles.Wordpress.com or believersingrace.com.

Except where otherwise indicated, all Scripture quotations in this book are taken from the King James Version of the Bible.

PRINTED IN THE UNITED STATES OF AMERICA

Dedication

I dedicate this book to my first grandchildren, Abraham and Moriah Flecksing. My God has promised me that He would pour out His spirit on my seed and my seed's seed, and that He would put His Words in your mouth. You two were the first of many precious gifts, and are called to lead the rest. May you absorb and live out the message of this little book. I love you both, very much–Grandpa Randles

> And the Redeemer shall come to Zion, and unto them that turn from transgression in Jacob, saith the Lord. As for me, this is my covenant with them, saith the Lord; My spirit that is upon thee, and my words which I have put in thy mouth, shall not depart out of thy mouth, nor out of the mouth of thy seed, nor out of the mouth of thy seed's seed, saith the Lord, from henceforth and for ever. (Isaiah 59:21)

I want to thank several who have helped in this endeavour. Jo and Glenn Stotz, thanks for your input. I also want to thank my incredibly talented nephew Zachariah Kulish for the painting that graces the cover, and for the rest of the cover, my talented brother Chuck Freitag. Thanks Sheryl Doonan for editing, and Karen Wilson for so much technical help. Above all else, I thank my lovely and patient wife Kristin, for without you I wouldn't be able to do what I do.

Contents

Chapter One
There Was a Pharisee

> There was a man of the Pharisees, named Nicodemus, a ruler of the Jews: The same came to Jesus by night, and said unto him, Rabbi, we know that thou art a teacher come from God: for no man can do these miracles that thou doest, except God be with him. (John 3:1-2)

John 3 is a classic Bible chapter. Jesus Himself is the instructor, and the subject is New Birth. The pupil, (standing in this passage as representative for all seekers of God), is a Senator of Israel, a Pharisee, a chief teacher of the Word of God and an expert on the Kingdom of God and entry into it. His name is Nicodemus.

Who were the Pharisees?

Over the years, there has developed a serious misconstruction about who these people were and how we are to view them. Modern readers of the Bible often see the Pharisees as real "bad guys", hypocritical to the core and vicious enemies of the Lord. The last thing anyone would want to be considered in modern evangelical

Christianity would be to be called a Pharisee.

The Pharisees that Jesus rebuked, exposed, and vehemently denounced in scripture seem to the modern Bible reader as an almost alien species. This is because we have developed caricatures of Pharisaism, which allow us to mentally distance ourselves from any identity with them. We may be a lot of things but we are certainly not greedy, hypocritical, murderous Pharisees!

But the Pharisees, and Jesus' encounter with them are meant to serve as a warning to us, for they apply particularly to we who are evangelicals. How could that be?

The Pharisees were the back to the Bible movement of the inter-testamental period! They sought to resist the worldliness that was sweeping away the majority of their countrymen in the ancient Jewish world.

That virulent species of worldliness was called "Hellenism", i.e. the acceptance of Greek culture, and the repudiation of Judaism. In an attempt at world unity, Hellenism was spread over the known world by Alexander the Great.

When Hellenism came into the Holy Land, many backslidden Jews adapted Hellenistic ways, some going as far as submitting to "reverse circumcisions"!

Later, in the days of the brutal prototype of the Anti-Christ, Antiochus Epiphanes, Hellenism was imposed by force on the remaining pious Jews. Sabbath observance was outlawed, there were forced "reverse circumcisions" and any mother who circumcised her child would be put to death. At one point even the High Priest of Israel took on a Greek name, and a gymnasium was built in Jerusalem. We are not talking about today's gyms for physical fitness. A "gymnasium" was a Greek school for the whole man. Athletic activities were done in the nude, Greek philosophy and the worship of the physical body were involved, and homosexuality was rampant.

Pharisaism emerged out of a godly resistance to all of that. The Pharisee attempted to take on his shoulders all of the 613 commands of the Law of God, making it his life's goal to keep them. He believed that by doing so, the Kingdom of God would come again to Israel.

The word Pharisee means "separated one". This was a serious reform movement within Judaism. By no means am I saying that I agree with what the Pharisees would end up as, nor do I deny that the Pharisees were the hypocrites Jesus exposed them to be. My purpose is to remove the caricature of them so that we can realize that God is not describing some openly hateful, alien cult to us, but rather people very much like the modern "back to the Bible" movement, concerned about worldliness and seeking to separate ourselves from it by turning to God and the Bible.

Actually, the Pharisees were theologically closest of all of the contemporary sects to Jesus. Unlike the ruling Sadducees, the Pharisees believed in death, resurrection, angels, demons, the afterlife, heaven and hell. The Pharisees were right on board with John the Baptist and Jesus at the beginning of Jesus' ministry. Because they were closest to him, Jesus critiqued them more than any other sect.

The many warnings to the Pharisees are meant as a message to all of us. Warnings against mere externalism, innovation, substitution of man-made precepts for the Word of God, eye service, self-seeking, and self-serving religion, misplaced emphasis, proof-texting, "using scripture" rather than truly seeking God, apply to every spiritual reform movement. The Pharisees were evangelical, crossing "land and sea" to make one convert!

This particular Pharisee served in the Sanhedrin, the Senate of Israel. He was a "chief ruler" and was called "The Teacher of Israel". His subject was the Kingdom of God and entry into it. Everyone esteemed him as a spiritual giant, and as a teacher of the nation.

But something about Jesus penetrated his heart, so the "teacher of Israel" went to meet him one evening.

Chapter Two
Born Again

> The same came to Jesus by night, and said unto Him, "Rabbi, we know that thou art a teacher come from God: for no man can do these miracles that thou doest, except God be with him." Jesus answered and said unto him, "Verily, verily, I say unto thee, except a man be born again, he cannot see the kingdom of God." (John 3: 2-3)

We have been looking at chapter 3 of the Gospel of John, a conversation between Jesus and a leading Pharisee, Nicodemus the *teacher of Israel.* The topic is the new birth, being born again.

We must appreciate the difficulties a man in his position faced, just to meet with Jesus. As a Sanhedrinist and chief Rabbi, he had immense obstacles to overcome, within his own soul and among his colleagues. That a well known religious leader would inquire of an untrained, itinerate country Rabbi would be scandalous. Small wonder he came by night!

The miracles Jesus performed had been sufficiently verified, that Nicodemus spoke for the other top rabbis and scholars of Israel as well as himself, when he said, "We know that you are a teacher sent from God . . ." (John 3:2).

Jesus didn't acknowledge this admission from Nicodemus and spoke directly to his expertise, the Kingdom of God and entrance into it.

> Verily, Verily I say unto you, unless a man be born again, he cannot see the Kingdom of God. (John 3:3)

As a Pharisee and as a Jew, Nicodemus held to a doctrine which taught that all Jews have a share in the life to come by virtue of being born of Abraham, Isaac, and Jacob. They believed that the Kingdom of God was a birthright of every Israelite. The Pharisees taught that,

> All Israelites have a share in the world to come. For it is written, "Thy people shall be all righteous, they shall inherit the land forever, the branch of my planting, the work of my hands, that I may be glorified." (Talmud, Sanhedrin 90a)

The refutation of this false doctrine was a major theme of John the Baptist's preaching, because this heresy was deluding the people of Israel into thinking they needed no repentance, though they were on the verge of a catastrophic judgment.

> . . . And think not to say within yourselves, "We have Abraham to our father." For I say unto you, that God is able of these stones to raise up children unto Abraham. (Matthew 3:9)

John railed against this delusion, warning those who listened that they were in danger of hell itself! Perhaps

Nicodemus himself was unnerved and convicted by John's preaching. Something shook him out of his complacency and drew him to Jesus. Isn't that why John the Baptist was sent? Was the Baptist not sent to prepare the hearts of men to accept Jesus?

Yet Jesus insists that the Israelite must be born again. The Jews did have a concept of born again, but Nicodemus knew that couldn't be what Jesus was referring to. A Bar Mitzvah is a *new birth* in Jewish thought.

For example: when a man became married, he was said to be *born again*, or should a man become ordained as a rabbi, he was born again. Also, the rabbis taught that should a man take upon his shoulders the Kingdom of God (for example, repent and come under God's government), he was said to be born again.

But Jesus insists that the opposite is true, a fallen man can't take upon his shoulders the Kingdom of God, in fact– ". . . unless you are born again, you can't even see the Kingdom of God".

A few verses later He will say, "unless one is born of water and the Spirit, he cannot enter the Kingdom of God." (John 3:5)

By calling for a new birth, Jesus is telling this proud Israelite, and all who will listen, that there is something inherently wrong with all of us, even the circumcised seed of Abraham. In our natural birth we are not good enough to enter into the kingdom of heaven.

Not only are we born blind to the kingdom of heaven, we are inherently born unfit, (Gentile or Jew) to enter into it! The law of God testifies of this.

Consider the commandments concerning physical birth. Circumcision presupposes guilt. The prescribed washings for ritual uncleanness for new mothers as well as laws which insist that firstborn males be redeemed, seem to say that; shame and sorrow are in conception and the transmission of seed, ever since the fall of man.

The Pharisees didn't hold to anything like our Christian teaching of original sin, at least not in their view of Israel. Had they paid closer attention to the Psalms, and other writings in their Bibles, they would have more readily accepted Jesus' call for a new birth.

> Behold, I was shapen in iniquity; and in sin did my mother conceive me. (Psalm 51:5)

> The wicked are estranged from the womb: they go astray as soon as they be born, speaking lies. (Psalm 58:3)

Chapter Three

Can a Man Be Born When He Is Old?

> Nicodemus saith unto him, How can a man be born when he is old? Can he enter the second time into his mother's womb, and be born? (John 3:4)

Jesus told Nicodemus, the Pharisee and *teacher of Israel* that he needed to be born again in order to see the Kingdom of God. By this time Nicodemus had already been born again in every way he knew how. In Jewish thought, as we said earlier, a man is said to be born again on the day of his Bar Mitzvah, or on the day he is married, or when ordained as a rabbi. Finally, should he fall away, on the day he fully repents he is said to be born again.

Jesus obviously talked to Nicodemus about something entirely unique to the Jewish idea of born again. Nicodemus correctly perceived that Jesus was telling him that he would have to virtually renounce his role as *teacher of Israel*, assume the role of a child and be willing to receive the basics of his faith as if he had never truly understood it. This is why Nicodemus asked:

> How can a man be born when he is old? Can he enter the second time into his mother's womb, and be born? (John 3:4)

The new birth presupposes the need to start over again. You can be born again. Your past can truly be past, your sins can be forgiven and by the gift of God you can live by a new principle of life from God called eternal life. As it is written:

> For the wages of sin is death; but the gift of God is eternal life through Jesus Christ our Lord. (Romans 6:23)

Nicodemus was no fool. He wasn't being sarcastic when he asked if a man could go back to his mother's womb. He was saying, *Can a man as invested in biblical religion as I am really start all over again? Are you saying that I need to go back to square one? Must I, the teacher of Israel take on again the role of a learner?*

It is one thing for the obviously ruined– prostitutes, drug addicts, pimps, and whoremongers, to see that they need a new start. To them, a message from heaven that we can be born again is truly glad news. What have they got to lose, but shame, sin, and remorse?

To someone as advanced and as esteemed as Nicodemus, so well regarded as an expert, and a righteous man esteemed among the proponents of that religion, to be told that he too has to be *born again* in the sense that Jesus was speaking, would require a tremendous amount of humility. What would a Nicodemus have to lose?

He would have much to lose in every worldly way. He would lose the honor and distinction of being a prime teacher of the only true religion on earth at that time, Judaism. The years he had invested in teaching, perhaps writing, and practicing Pharisaism, the strictest sect of Judaism, and all of the honors and self satisfaction and sense of righteous accomplishment that goes with it.

Yet Jesus tells him that he, Nicodemus, must be born again to even see the Kingdom of God? Nicodemus was considered an expert on the Kingdom of God, a guide to others, a Bible teacher. Sometime after Nicodemus, another Pharisee, Saul of Tarsus, was rising rapidly among the sect, surpassing all the other Pharisees in zeal, and piety. But then Jesus found him and brought him to the same crisis as Nicodemus.

Could he start over? Would he renounce his own *righteousness*? Here is his own account:

> For we are the circumcision, which worship God in the spirit, and rejoice in Christ Jesus, and have no confidence in the flesh. Though I might also have confidence in the flesh. If any other man thinketh that he hath whereof he might trust in the flesh, I more: Circumcised the eighth day, of the stock of Israel, of the tribe of Benjamin, an Hebrew of the Hebrews; as touching the law, a Pharisee; Concerning zeal, persecuting the church; touching the righteousness which is in the law, blameless. But what things were gain to me, those I counted loss for Christ. Yea doubtless, and I count all things but loss for the excellency

> of the knowledge of Christ Jesus my Lord: for whom I have suffered the loss of all things, and do count them but dung, that I may win Christ, And be found in him, not having mine own righteousness, which is of the law, but that which is through the faith of Christ, the righteousness which is of God by faith. (Philippians 3:3-9)

It is easy to let go of the ugly residue of sin– the shame, disease, reproach, and so on.

But other aspects of sin bring to mind a verse about Moses, which involves renouncing the honors, the connections, the accomplishments and points of pride referred to biblically as, *confidence in the flesh.*

> By faith Moses, when he was come to years, refused to be called the son of Pharaoh's daughter; Choosing rather to suffer affliction with the people of God, than to enjoy the pleasures of sin for a season; Esteeming the reproach of Christ greater riches than the treasures in Egypt: for he had respect unto the recompense of the reward. (Hebrews 11:24-26)

It is not just the *bad* of our life, that we must renounce, but even the *good,* for none of our own *goodness* is sufficient to commend us to the Holy God before whom we must give an account. Those areas in our lives of which Paul said, we *put confidence in the flesh,* and hold to *a righteousness of our own* fall short of His standard and are abominable to God.

It is incredibly difficult for the Nicodemuses among us to renounce their own self-righteousness. For many it is the obstacle to submitting to and accepting the new birth. Only God could show us that it is not just the things we do that condemns us, but it is who we are. We can't be *improved*; we must be born again!

Therefore the answer to the question of Nicodemus, and to every other future Nicodemus, Saul of Tarsus, Mary Magdalene, Simon the Leper, C. S. Lewis, or any other sinner, great or small, *good* or evil, respectable or utterly ruined, is the same. Can a man be born when he is old?

The answer is "**Definitely**!" According to Jesus, we can start over, we can begin anew, we can be born again, but only by receiving the gift of God, which is eternal life through Jesus.

Chapter Four
Born of Water and of Spirit

> Jesus answered, Verily, verily, I say unto thee, Except a man be born of water and of the Spirit, he cannot enter into the kingdom of God. That which is born of the flesh is flesh; and that which is born of the Spirit is spirit. Marvel not that I said unto thee, Ye must be born again. (John 3:5-7)

John 3 is the record of an interview, between the great rabbi and Pharisee, Nicodemus, and the non formally trained, itinerant Rabbi from Nazareth, Jesus. But Jesus is the one who is teaching Nicodemus and through him, He is teaching all men. The subject is the *New Birth*.

The Jews had a concept of new birth but it was non-biblical and inadequate. Their concept was merely a colloquialism for any initiation into new responsibilities, such as marriage or initiation into ministry.

Perhaps a bit closer to the true sense that Jesus uses, the Jews believed that if a defector from faith repented, he was said to be *born again*.

But Jesus is obviously calling for something far deeper.

Jesus insists that all men, regardless of circumcision, works, religious attainment, or whether or not he is of the seed of Abraham, needs to be reborn to so much as see the kingdom of heaven, let alone enter into it. According to Jesus, the new birth is a matter of ultimate and final salvation, without it there is no entry into God's kingdom.

Jesus indeed is the Lord of Glory, but in the days of His flesh, He was a Rabbi, who taught the Word of God. He went by scripture, and never said anything at all that wasn't either a direct quotation, or a direct allusion to the scriptures.

As a man, Jesus held the scripture in the highest regard. When tempted by the devil, He said, "*It is written* . . ." appealing to the Word of God, and not applying His own thoughts and feelings, thus putting Himself under the authority of scripture. In His humanity, Jesus did not live His life according to His own thoughts and feelings, He lived by the Word of God.

This is important to note, because there is much confusion about verse 5, "unless a man is born of water and Spirit, he can't enter into the Kingdom of God . . ."

Many believe that Jesus referred to both water baptism and spirit baptism, in talking to Nicodemus. The uniquely Christian baptism for the remission of sins was not inaugurated until after Calvary, where Jesus died for our sins. The same goes for being *Spirit Baptized.* John 7:37-38 tells us that there could be no Spirit Baptism until Jesus was "glorified".

Nicodemus would have no idea what being *Spirit*

Baptized meant, so I doubt it was a reference to that.

Others believe that Jesus is contrasting natural and spiritual birth. But why would He need to tell us that we must be born naturally? It doesn't ring true that Jesus would need to state the obvious.

I believe that Jesus talked in terms that Nicodemus as a rabbi, a Sanhedrinist and an expert in scripture would know well, for Jesus was alluding to a specific scripture, Ezekiel 36:24-27.

> For I will take you from among the heathen, and gather you out of all countries, and will bring you into your own land. Then will I sprinkle clean water upon you, and ye shall be clean: from all your filthiness, and from all your idols, will I cleanse you. A new heart also will I give you, and a new spirit will I put within you: and I will take away the stony heart out of your flesh, and I will give you an heart of flesh. And I will put my spirit within you, and cause you to walk in my statutes, and ye shall keep my judgments, and do them.

Hearing this, Nicodemus would have known instantly that Jesus referred to the promise of God to Israel, from the days of the Babylonian captivity, that God would one day bring them back into the land in unbelief, and would cure the nation once and for all of their penchant for idolatry.

The LORD would effect this for Israel, by "washing them with water", and by removing from them their "stoney heart", replacing it with a new heart, sensitive again to God, a heart to follow and obey God. This would happen when God put His Spirit in them.

The promise of God to Israel was that He would renew the nation by water and Spirit, (for example, washing and regeneration). To Nicodemus and his contemporaries, Ezekiel's promise had been fulfilled in the days of the return from exile, hundreds of years earlier.

Had not Israel already repudiated idolatry? But what is idolatry but alienation from God in the heart and the replacement of God himself with man-made images.

By the time of Jesus and John the Baptist, Judaism had evolved into an intense purification religion. The emphasis of rabbis, scribes and Pharisees was separation and the removal of defilement.

Jesus had warned them however that the heart itself was the very fountain of all defilement, and that defilement is not external, but springs from a fallen nature.

> There is nothing from without a man, that entering into him can defile him: but the things which come out of him, those are they that defile the man . . . And he said, That which cometh out of the man, that defileth the man. For from within, out of the heart of men, proceed evil thoughts, adulteries, fornications, murders, Thefts, covetousness, wickedness, deceit, lasciviousness, an evil eye, blasphemy, pride, foolishness: All these evil things come from within, and defile the man. (Mark 7:15, 20-23)

A close reading of the Gospel of John reveals that untold gallons of water had to be made available for the manifold ceremonial washings required not only by the law of Moses, but by the traditions of the elders also.

Obviously purification alone is inadequate. Our need goes deeper than the removal of defilement. We need new life! Nothing less than a resurrection will meet our deepest, spiritual need. Only an act of God Himself can remake us, only God can raise the dead.

We do need to be forgiven, and washed clean of the things we have done against God and man. But washing alone fails to meet our deepest need, for our problem is not just what we have done, but who we are before God.

Because we are all dead to God, we all need a spiritual New Birth! God offers to make us all over again, to give us a new heart. We can receive a moral and spiritual renovation from God by accepting Jesus.

> But as many as received him, to them gave he power to become the sons of God, even to them that believe on his name: Which were born, not of blood, nor of the will of the flesh, nor of the will of man, but of God. (John 1:12-13)

Chapter Five
Born From Above

> That which is born of the flesh is flesh; and that which is born of the Spirit is spirit. Marvel not that I said unto thee, Ye must be born again. The wind bloweth where it listeth, and thou hearest the sound thereof, but canst not tell whence it cometh, and whither it goeth: so is every one that is born of the Spirit. (John 3:6-8)

The Apostle John likes to use words in his gospel that have two meanings, both of which apply to the word in the text. For example, in John 11 when Lazarus died, Jesus told the disciples that "*Lazarus sleeps*". Of course Lazarus had died, but he died in fellowship with Jesus. Which is it? Death or sleep? In Christ death is sleep. Though believers may die physically, death to us is sleep.

In the same manner, the text in John 3 uses the metaphor of the wind blowing, in speaking of the moving of the Holy Spirit in the divine act of new birth. The word used for *wind* is the same word as the word for *Spirit.*

The Spirit blows where it wants to, "The wind blows where it listeth . . ." The same goes for the phrase "*born again*", (Greek *Gennatha Anothen*).

The phrase means both *born again*, and *born from above*. Both apply to the teaching of Jesus. We are called to start all over again, by the power of the Holy Spirit, and to live by a heavenly principle of life, a gift called *Eternal Life*.

The new birth is something imparted to us as a gift from God. It is a work of the Holy Spirit, who proceeds from the Father and the Son. Eternal Life cannot be imparted to anyone by man.

> But as many as received him, to them gave he power to become the sons of God, even to them that believe on his name: Which were born, not of blood, nor of the will of the flesh, nor of the will of man, but of God. (John 1:12-13)

In all of the years I have been a Pastor at Believers in Grace Fellowship (since 1982), as a church or as individuals, we have never created one Christian! Not once in all of our time of existence, have we ever caused anyone to be *born again*.

The new birth is an act of God! It is an impartation of the life of God to a sinner who has received Jesus Christ, the seed of God. The Holy Spirit alone brings the sinner to that point, convicting and enlightening and imparting to whosoever believes in eternal life. That is a share in the life of Jesus.

> Jesus said that; "It is the spirit that quickeneth; the flesh profiteth nothing: the words that I speak unto you, they are spirit, and they are life." (John 6:63)

That is why the apostle Peter reminds us that we

have been ". . . born again, not of corruptible seed, but of incorruptible, by the word of God, which liveth and abideth for ever." (1 Peter 1:23)

When Jesus compared the flesh and the Spirit, (That which is flesh is flesh, and that which is Spirit is Spirit), He wasn't talking about the difference between sinful and holy. Rather, He uses the expression flesh to denote that which is frail, finite and earthly, versus that which is of a heavenly origin.

Paul elaborates on the difference between "that which is of flesh" versus "that which is of the Spirit" by contrasting those born of Adam (flesh), and those born anew, of Christ (Spirit).

Every human being has descended from, and has received by birth, the (fallen and corrupt) nature of our father, Adam. This is the first birth, and it is one that renders us unfit, and inadequate to inherit the kingdom of heaven.

No matter how vile, sinful, or lofty and noble he is, a son of Adam is a son of Adam. He is already fallen, sinful, estranged from God, with a corruptible nature, and liable to a deserved damnation. He may be religious, but if unregenerate, he is dead to the only true God. No amount of goodness can undo that, for in God's sight, "there is none good, no not one. . ."

But when he receives a second birth, when he is *born from above* by receiving the gift of God, through the incorruptible seed of the gospel, that person becomes a partaker of the nature of God. He comes alive to God, now able to commune with his Maker. He is said to be *begotten of God.*

> Whosoever believeth that Jesus is the Christ is born of God: and every one that loveth him that begat loveth him also that is begotten of him. (1 John 5:1)

He passes out of the *Adam's* family, and has escaped the judgment. On the cross Jesus bore his judgment, and made Himself responsible for the sins of all who would believe in Him. As Paul says:

> For since by man came death, by man came also the resurrection of the dead. For as in Adam all die, even so in Christ shall all be made alive. (1 Corinthians 15:21-22)

How does one leave a family? If we were *born* into *Adam's* family, how then do we exit? We must die; it's the only way out of a family!

By the gospel we believe that we have already died, when we acknowledged our sinfulness, and gave up on our own self-righteousness, to call upon the crucified and risen Lord Jesus! Our baptism was our funeral, and as we were raised up out of the water, Christ has raised us from the dead unto a new heavenly life! We are *born again* unto a living hope by the resurrection from the dead!

I don't like bumper sticker theology normally, but I saw one that really did say it well one time: *If you are only born once, you will die twice, but if you are born twice, you will only die once!*

Chapter Six

How Can These Things Be? (Unbelief)

> Nicodemus answered and said unto him, How can these things be? Jesus answered and said unto him, Art thou a master of Israel, and knowest not these things? Verily, verily, I say unto thee, We speak that we do know, and testify that we have seen; and ye receive not our witness. If I have told you earthly things, and ye believe not, how shall ye believe, if I tell you of heavenly things? (John 3:9-12)

The third chapter of John allows us in on a conversation between Jesus and one of the great rabbis of Israel, the Pharisee and Sanhedrinist, Nicodemus. The topic is the Kingdom of God and entry into it. Jesus' teaching is that a *new birth* is necessary to enter into the kingdom, or to even see it.

Jesus has thus far taught, that the *new birth* is a revelation from God, an enablement to see the *Kingdom of God*, and to enter into it. It is a work of the sovereign Spirit of God. (The wind blows where it listeth).

The new birth is nothing less than the renewal promised to the returning captives of Israel, in the Book of Ezekiel, when God said; "I will wash you with water" and "I will take out of you a heart of stone, and put within you a new heart of flesh". Furthermore, God said to them; "I will put my Spirit within you".

Nicodemus was well versed in Ezekiel, and the prophets and law of God, having dedicated his whole life to learning and teaching them. But at this point in the discussion he raises an objection, "How can these things be?".

It is instructive to note the way Jesus handled this objection, for almost universally, the world objects to the call for and promise of a new birth from God!

The objection of Nicodemus pleads ignorance, but Jesus isn't going to allow that, especially from the *Master of Israel*, that is, the supreme rabbi. To loosely paraphrase Jesus' reply–

> Are you telling me you don't know these things? . . . You, The expert in the law of God are going to plead ignorance of this basic promise and the need it presupposes?

What things are Nicodemus pretending to not know?

The promise of a new heart for Israel, and the idea that it was needed. The implications of this promise in Ezekiel, long anticipated by Moses and the other prophets, that God would *circumcise Israel's hearts, and write His law on them*, presupposed that Israel's heart was not right with God as it was, and the truth that not all Israel is Israel, and finally, that circumcision must be of the heart.

These promises also inferred the utter inadequacy

of the law to fit the nation for the kingdom, that is, the rule of God. Nicodemus would have been all too familiar with scripture such as:

> And the LORD thy God will circumcise thine heart, and the heart of thy seed, to love the LORD thy God with all thine heart, and with all thy soul, that thou mayest live. (Deuteronomy 30:6)
>
> Then will I sprinkle clean water upon you, and ye shall be clean: from all your filthiness, and from all your idols, will I cleanse you. A new heart also will I give you, and a new spirit will I put within you: and I will take away the stony heart out of your flesh, and I will give you an heart of flesh. And I will put my spirit within you, and cause you to walk in my statutes, and ye shall keep my judgments, and do them. (Ezekiel 36:25-27)
>
> Behold, the days come, saith the LORD, that I will make a new covenant with the house of Israel, and with the house of Judah: Not according to the covenant that I made with their fathers in the day that I took them by the hand to bring them out of the land of Egypt; which my covenant they brake, although I was an husband unto them, saith the LORD: But this shall be the covenant that I will make with the house of Israel; After those days, saith the LORD, I will put my law in their inward parts, and write it in their hearts; and will be their God, and they shall be my people. (Jeremiah 31:31-33)

It would be humbling for any Israelite to truly accept these promises with all that they imply– Israel's hardness of heart, her deadness to God, the inadequacy of formal adherence to the law of God, and Israel's lovelessness. Truly dealing with these promises would inevitably lead to the recognition of the *new birth*.

Why doesn't Nicodemus, Israel's teacher, and typical representative of all of Israel's sages, see what Jesus is calling for? Not merely because of ignorance, but rather an obstinate and willful blindness. Jesus puts His finger on it in His reply to Nicodemus.

> We speak that we do know, and testify that we have seen; and ye **receive not** our witness. If I have told you earthly things, and ye **believe not**, how shall ye believe, if I tell you of heavenly things?

Nicodemus cannot seem to receive the testimony of the word of God, that Israel's kingdom will not be realized until she is given a *new heart* by God, (earthly things).

But Israel is a microcosm of all of humanity. How then would Nicodemus be able to accept the broader revelation that all men everywhere, Jew and/or Gentile, must be born again by the Holy Spirit to enter into the (heavenly) kingdom?

So it is with man. Particularly in the case of the wise and learned, rather than being a matter of *not knowing*, man's real problem is unbelief, which is willful ignorance! The refusal to accept the implications of Jesus' gospel of a new life, bars millions from the way to heaven.

Hell itself echoes with the endless rationalizations of unbelief, such as; "If I believed that, I would be admitting I was wrong all this time?" and "If I accept that I would have to admit I was a sinner!" or "Too many people look up to me as a 'good moral person' for me to become as a child and start all over again." I told one man he needed to be born again, and his reply was; "Why should I when I got it right the first time?" The difference between unbelief and ignorance is the difference between not knowing, and refusing to know. Ignorance can be cured, but unbelief requires repentance, for it is a serious moral problem, a sin against God.

Chapter Seven
He that Came Down from Heaven

> And no man hath ascended up to heaven, but he that came down from heaven, even the Son of man which is in heaven." (John 3:13)

Nicodemus was a religious leader, the *Rabbi of Israel.* But he was drawn to seek out the obvious wisdom of an "untrained" itinerant Rabbi, Jesus of Nazareth. It was the miracles of Jesus, as well as His teaching, that compelled Nicodemus and other leading Rabbis to acknowledge that God was with him.

Jesus wasted no time at all in the interview, informing Nicodemus that he would have to be born again to be able to see or even enter the Kingdom of God. Indeed, contrary to Nicodemus' belief, the nation Israel, had yet to realize Ezekiel's prophecy that God would give her a new heart.

But as most people do, Nicodemus balked, he feigned ignorance. The proud heart of fallen man is loath to admit that he needs a new birth.

Perhaps he will admit to the need of a little improvement here or there, but to become as a dependent child and start all over again? Maybe a prostitute or a swindling tax collector needs to be born again, but a proud Pharisee, noted for his piety?

Thus Jesus takes Nicodemus, and all of us, to the very heart of our problem, which is unbelief. This subtle sin perverts even *true* religion, rendering it the very antithesis of that for which it was intended by God.

At the core of all false religion is a spiritual fallacy. This fallacy runs through Hinduism, Islam, The New Age movement, and the modern secular religions such as evolution, socialism, and communism. Furthermore, it undergirds the seed of false Christianity.

~~~~~

If man is going to be saved at all, God Himself is going to have to come down to us.

~~~~~

The false premise is that man can rise up, from the earth, by his own spiritual efforts and become *as gods*, as the serpent promised our first father and mother, Adam and Eve. This belief is, to the human race, like an incurable spiritual disease. Man has always been drawn to religion that tells him that man can be god. No matter how hellish the results, man cannot let go of this belief.

This premise is called the mystery of iniquity, in 2 Thessalonians 2– "*For the mystery of iniquity doth already work. . .*"

Mankind's sad history will culminate in the final expression of this false belief, for there is prophesied to arise a man of sin who will seem to be the realization of this dark ideal.

He is the "man of sin", the champion of a world which has succumbed fully to this evil premise. His public demeanor is prophetically described as an ongoing illustration of this sinful mystery.

> Who opposeth and exalteth himself above all that is called God, or that is worshipped; so that he as God sitteth in the temple of God, shewing himself that he is God. (2 Thessalonians 2:3-7)

Look at the miserable *utopias* of the last century! The new *scientific* man was going to rise up and make his own earthly paradise. He was going to be more equitable, more merciful, and more just then God Himself! This is the actual principle underneath all of man's religious history.

Pyramids and ziggurats that have been built on every continent are but religious aspirations, *steps to ascent* unto godhood, degrees of advancement man made, but devil inspired religious expression. Judaism itself, as it developed in the days of Nicodemus and the Rabbis and sages, degenerated to this false principle of advancement by the works of the law of God.

Those underneath this system wearied themselves in the never-ending toil in pursuit of the goal, which was to be able to *ascend to heaven* by their good deeds.

This is why Jesus addressed Himself to them as *weary and heavy laden*, in Matthew 11–

> Come unto me, all ye that labour and are heavy laden, and I will give you rest. Take my yoke upon you, and learn of me; for I am meek and lowly in heart: and ye shall find rest unto your souls. (Matthew 11:28-29)

This was the error of Nicodemus' generation, a distortion of biblical religion, a religion of works of righteousness, self redemption, an attempt to *ascend unto heaven.*

Nicodemus and his generation are not the only ones who fall into this error. Self salvation by works is the default position of most of the world, to whom the Savior makes this simple but ultimate statement: "No man has ascended to Heaven . . ."

No one. Not even the greatest sage! Not Mother Teresa, not Gandhi, not the most benevolent philanthropist. Human religion cannot save anyone! There is none righteous, no not one . . . by the works of the law shall no flesh be justified!

If the false religion of self effort, known biblically as the "mystery of iniquity" is the undying, rebellious faith that man can ascend, and "become as gods", what then is the true spirituality?

> And without controversy great is the mystery of godliness: God was manifest in the flesh . . . (1 Timothy 3:16)

> . . . but he that came down from heaven, even the Son of man. (John 3:13)

No, man isn't going to "rise up" and become as little "gods". Man has been ruined by his fall from fellowship with God. He is too spiritually and morally bankrupt, and is not fit as he is in his fallen state to enter the kingdom of heaven. He is powerless, and impotent, he is blind, lame and *dead in his trespasses and sins.*

If man is going to be saved at all, God Himself is going to have to come down to us. The Son of Man is going to have to descend, there is going to have to be an incarnation.

One of these two spiritualities is very exalting to man, it promotes his sense of pride, independence and accomplishment. The other is very humiliating, for man must admit to his own impotence, he must confess his sin, it doesn't boost his *self- esteem.* Which one will be the *popular religion*? Which one will most of humanity embrace, other than an intervention of grace? Who wants to be a wretch (as in Amazing Grace) when you can still believe in yourself?

Chapter Eight
How God Loved the World

> For God so loved the world, that he gave his only begotten Son, that whosoever believeth in him should not perish, but have everlasting life. (John 3:16)

We find ourselves at this point in our study of John chapter 3 at perhaps the most beloved and well-known verse in the Bible. Certainly, it is the singularly most widely translated sentence of any kind in the world. With reverence we approach these words of glad tidings from heaven.

But it is possible, in fact probable, that the sheer familiarity of these words to many in our culture, has an unfortunate deadening effect, rather than the one intended by the gracious Savior who first uttered them.

For example, nearly everyone can quote John 3:16 these days, but how many can quote John 3:14-15, or John 3:17-21?

This beautiful verse has a context, and can only truly be understood by putting it within the flow of thought that preceded it.

For example, even the words *for* and *so* in the verse have an important meaning. "For God so loved the world . . ."

Obviously, the word in the verse, *for*, would refer to what had been said up to that point. For example–the discussion about the new birth (Ezekiel 36), the new heart and the washing that God would give Israel, as well as to the immediate context, the story of the brass serpent in Numbers 21.

The word *for* of John 3:16 points to the teaching of John 3:14-15.

> And as Moses lifted up the serpent in the wilderness, even so must the Son of man be lifted up: That whosoever believeth in him should not perish, but have eternal life . . . For God so loved the world . . . (John 3:14-16)

The word *so,* is also very much misunderstood by many modern readers, for the tendency is to interpret it as a description of intensity– "God so loved the world . . . i.e., He loved the world so much . . ."

I gained what I believe to be an insight into this verse, in a little book[1] by a British Bible teacher, David Pawson. He pointed out that the word *so* should be placed before the word *God.* In other words, it should read: "For so God loved the world . . ."

It could be justifiably read, "In this way God loved the world . . . " or "In thus manner did God love the

1 *Is John 3:16 The Gospel?*, David Pawson, Terra Nova Publications.

world."

In what manner? God loved the whole world in the same way He loved Israel when snakes were killing them in the wilderness!

We have to ask ourselves what was happening in Numbers 21 that Jesus says gives us an insight into how God loved the world?

Because of the people's sin of ingratitude and unbelief (they had been murmuring against God and threatened to kill Moses and Aaron), a judgment fell in the form of poisonous snakes being sent to bite and kill the rebellious Israelites. People were dropping right and left, but like Christ, Moses and Aaron fell on their knees and interceded for them.

What was God's instruction?

They were to make a brass serpent and erect it on a pole, and hold it up publicly, telling the people that whoever looks up to that serpent would live!

According to Jesus, that is exactly how God loved the world.

He didn't wipe out the serpents, though people all around were dying of snakebite. God didn't organize the people into serpent killing groups, nor did He call on them to go back into their own past to see where they had gone wrong.

He didn't indulge the rebels, *eradicating* all that was harming them, leaving them as they were.

What did God do to *love the world*? He gave them a way out!

He lifted up a *cross* for them to see. Brass is a metal

that symbolizes divine judgment. For example, when Israel wouldn't obey the Lord, God told them there would be "brass heavens", for He wouldn't answer their prayers.

The serpent is the great enemy of mankind, but in the offering of Jesus, the serpent came under God's judgment, and death itself died.

> Now is the judgment of this world, now shall the prince of this world be cast down, and If I be lifted up from the earth I will draw all men unto me. (John 12)

Saving faith involves a believing look.

The people of Israel were required to look away from their snakebites, from their neighbors and their past, and to gaze upon the God-appointed, lifted up brass serpent in order to be healed.

Even so the people of the earth are required to look by faith at the Son of God, lifted up, bearing our judgment upon the tree. By death, *destroying death* for us, Jesus set us free from the mortal snakebite of our sins.

> For as much then as the children are partakers of flesh and blood, he also himself likewise took part of the same; that through death he might destroy him that had the power of death, that is, the devil; And deliver them who through fear of death were all their lifetime subject to bondage. (Hebrews 2:14-15)

This love of God is amazing! In view of the cross of Jesus it would be blasphemy to question it, or to deny the goodness of God which he displayed once and for all on Calvary. But it is not *unconditional love.*

The serpents are still biting rebellious sinners, people are still perishing and going to the eternal judgment that they deserve. Nor has God removed the snakes or the fires of hell.

But in Jesus, He has given us a way out; He has made for us a *righteous* way of escape. A holy God has made a *holy* way for us sinners to come into His *holy* heaven. We are to look away from ourselves and our situation and with trembling faith and worship, look upon Jesus in faith and worship unto Him, crucified and lifted up as our substitute.

Chapter Nine

The World that God Loved

> For God so Loved the World that He gave his only begotten Son, that whosoever believeth on Him might not perish, but have everlasting life. (John 3:16)

John 3:16 is perhaps the most universally recognized verse in all of scripture. When a famous athlete in American professional football, named Tim Tebow, put the address John 3:16 on his blackening paint (under his eyes), Google reported that there were 92 million hits looking for John 3:16.

I think it is a great thing that John 3:16 has gotten so much attention, and for so long. It is a tremendous summary of the essence of the gospel. *"For God so loved the world . . ."*

Let us consider the phrase, *the world* as it is used in scripture, for it is the direct object of God's love. But what do we mean by the expression, "the world"?

Scripture uses the phrase in more than one way. There are times when the word refers to the physical earth, as in "God made the world . . .". However, it is obvious that John 3:16 isn't referring to the earth.

In other places the phrase, *the world* is a reference to the present *age*. In that case, the Greek word is completely different from the verses in John. It is the word *aeon* (age). For example, Galatians 1:4 says,

> Grace be to you and peace from God the Father, and from our Lord Jesus Christ, Who gave himself for our sins, that he might deliver us from this present evil world. (Galatians 1:4)

However, the term the *world* in John 3:16 refers to the entirety of humanity, estranged from God, and lost in sin. "God so Loved the World".

The Greek word for world is *cosmos*, means *order* or *adornment*. It has to do with the ways fallen man has developed spiritually, intellectually and culturally without God. The world hates God and always has . . . but God loved the world.

This world that God loved is further described in scripture as a spiritual entity. Since the fall, man has been without God, utterly estranged from God and in truth, at enmity with the Creator. Man always fights and resists God.

Consider just a sampling of what the Bible tells us about the nature of the world, that God has loved.

> If the world hate you, ye know that it hated me before it hated you. If ye were of the world, the world would love his own: but because ye are not of the world, but I have chosen you out of the world, therefore the world hateth you. (John 15:18-19)

> He was in the world, and the world was made by him, and the world knew him not. (John 1:10)

> Even the Spirit of truth; whom the world cannot receive . . . (John 14:17)

> Hereafter I will not talk much with you: for the prince of this world cometh, and hath nothing in me. (John 14:31)

We are told that the world hates Christ, and would not receive Him, neither can it receive the Holy Spirit of truth. It also hates Christians and persecutes them.

Finally, the Word of God reveals that the "prince of this world" is Satan himself, and that the whole world lies in the power of the wicked one! (1 John 5:19)

In other words, all of the diverse forms of *religion* that have developed in the world, outside of the revelation of God in Christ, amounts to a form of humanism, and ultimately, Satan worship. We emphasize, with Jesus, that "God so loved the world . . .", describing the divine love, not as a feeling or a passion, but as an act, an event in time and space, an occurrence in history. When did God love the world? He loved it once (and for all) at Calvary, when He gave His Son as an offering for our sins.

That is when God "loved" the world.

At Calvary, God loved a world that has always hated and rejected Him. This is a world that is inveterate in its hatred for God. This is a world that murmurs, complains, and calls God's righteousness, and love into question constantly.

Yet God loved the world, in a specific and focused way. Not in a general way, did He love the world, but specifically and on His own terms.

God didn't love the world *unconditionally* in the sense of God *seeing good* in the world in spite of its flaws. In fact He has judged the world already, the sentence is passed, the Lord will execute His wrath upon this world. God knows that this world is in deep rebellion against Him. Yet knowing the truth about this evil age, God yet loved the world, giving us a way of salvation.

There can be no profitable experience of God's love, outside of the full acceptance of Jesus' offering at Calvary, with all of its ramifications. God cannot be known outside of the cross of Jesus Christ.

Chapter Ten

The Nature of God's Love for the World

> For God so loved the world that He gave his only begotten Son, that whosoever believes on Him might not perish but have everlasting life. (John 3:16)

Because of the influence of modernism, and of psychology upon the biblical understanding of many, even in evangelicalism, the whole concept of the love of God has been distorted. People import their own humanistic understanding of what love is, into texts such as John 3:16.

For example, many modern pastors and teachers say something to the effect that the cross shows us the measure of our value. As one popular Christian teacher put it,

> There must be something truly wonderful about us if God can love us and accept us so readily.

Another otherwise very effective apologist assures us that: "You are 'worth Jesus' to God because that is what he paid for you." [2]

We have all heard views such as this, or variations of it such as the following from another popular evangelical author, who posits that,

> Of course, the greatest demonstration of a person's worth to God was shown in giving us his Son. [3]

I believe that perspectives such as these are misleading. Though they contain partial truth, the emphasis of these statements is skewed, leading people to a distorted understanding of the love of God.

As Martin Luther helpfully said,

> God didn't love us because we are valuable, we become valuable because God chose to love us!

What did Jesus really mean when He proclaimed that God so loved the world?

To understand this we must first grasp the biblical meaning of the word *love*. In the Greek language of the New Testament, there is more than one word for *love*.

The Greek word *eros*, from which we obtain the word *erotic*, means the love of desire. The young man says to the young girl, *I love you*, but often what he means is *I want you . . . (for me!)*.

---

2 Josh McDowell, *Building Your Self- Esteem* (Wheaton: Tyndale, 1986), pp. 42-43.

3 William Kirwin, *Biblical Concepts for Christian Counseling* (Grand Rapids: Baker, 1984), p. 107.

There is a valid eros, within the bonds of holy matrimony, but we live in a society of eroticism that is inordinate, promiscuous and unholy.

There is another Greek word translated *love*, *phileo* which means, the *love of a brother*, or of *friendship*. The city *Philadelphia* means *city of brotherly love*. A *Francophile* is someone who loves that which is French.

There is yet another Greek word, *storge*, which refers to affection, but it can vary in the spectrum of commitment. *Storge* can and should be part of what parents feel towards their children. *Storge* also refers, in various degrees, to the different levels of natural affection for those God has put into our lives.

But *storge* can even mean something like what our modern word *cuteness* means, the feeling one gets when they see a pretty baby, or a child. God did not "storge the world" in John 3:16.

The God of John 3:16 did not love the world, based on something within us that was desirable to Him, or because there was something in us that He saw that was good, noble or even likable. Certainly His love for us should not be interpreted as a measurement of how *worthy* we were.

God didn't love the world according to sentimental affection either.

The word Jesus used in John 3:16 is *agape*. Agape refers to the love of the will. In spite of the animosity and rebellion of man against God, He saw our need, and willed our good. Agape moved Him to do what was necessary to save us from the wrath we deserved.

You could say, He set his love on us, while we were yet sinners.

That God should "Love the World" which has rejected and despised Him, and when given the chance, crucified Him, is the greatest story ever told! It is incomprehensible!

But many in this day are like the French atheist, who upon his deathbed was asked, "What if you find out that you were wrong?"

His nonchalant answer, "God will forgive me, that is his job . . . no?"

God did love the world, amazingly enough, so much that He found a righteous way to satisfy the claims of his Holy justice against us, while at the time showing his infinite mercy to us. The answer to the dilemma? The cross of Jesus.

> For he hath made him to be sin for us, who knew no sin; that we might be made the righteousness of God in him. (2 Corinthians 5:21)

Chapter Eleven

God's Love is an Awesome Mystery

> For God so loved the world that He gave his only begotten Son, that whosoever believes on Him might not perish but have everlasting life. (John 3:16)

> But God, who is rich in mercy, for his great love wherewith he loved us . . . (Ephesians 2:4)

John 3 is the record of an interview that Jesus gave to a leading rabbi, a senator (Sanhedrinist) and a Pharisee, Nicodemus. The topic? The New Birth.

Jesus told Nicodemus that the *new birth* was more than the acceptance of a new set of responsibilities such as marriage or ministry, as the Jews believed. The *new birth* is an act of God , the Holy Spirit. It was and is the fulfillment of the promise given through Ezekiel, that God would grant Israel a "washing in water" and give them a new "tender heart of flesh" that they might keep His commands.

No human being could ever become good enough to attain this new birth, it is a gift of God, given to us by the descent of the "Son of Man which is in heaven", but who has come to the earth.

The gift of the New Birth would come as a result of an event akin to Moses' "brass serpent", lifted up in the wilderness. Even so must the "*son of man be lifted up*", that those who believe in him might receive the gift of eternal life. The Son would bear the judgment that we deserved, on the tree, that we might live.

We discussed previously what is not meant by the phrase "*For God so loved the world*". We had to because decades of humanistic teachings, the influence of psychology and the increasing sentimentalization of Christianity, have led to serious misconceptions about God's love.

God did not love the world because of something which He saw that was *desirable* in it. Nor is the cross the measure of our worth as so many in this psychologized age assert. There was nothing in us at all that compelled God to love the world.

The word for love in John 3:16 is *agape*, and it means that God chose to love us, He willed it, and set His love upon us, solely because of who He is, not who we are.

God saw our plight, chose to will our good, and did what needed to be done, to save us. There are many facets to this, *love so amazing, and so Divine*, in fact it would take eternity to even begin to plumb the depths of the love Jesus mentioned in John 3:16.

Let it suffice us for now to look at just a few of them. What was it in God that compelled Him to offer up His Son for our salvation?

Mercy - The God revealed by Jesus in John 3 is a God of mercy and truth. He doesn't wish for anyone to perish, as the apostle Peter says, but that all might come to repentance, and receive the gift of God which is everlasting life.

His very nature is forgiveness, as the Psalmist indicates–

> The LORD is merciful and gracious, slow to anger, and plenteous in mercy. He will not always chide: neither will he keep his anger for ever. He hath not dealt with us after our sins; nor rewarded us according to our iniquities. For as the heaven is high above the earth, so great is his mercy toward them that fear him. (Psalm 103:8-11)

The mercy of God compels Him to want to relieve the sufferings even of those justly afflicted. He saw our sin, and with it all of its implications, all of the misery, shame, pain, confusion and death that the aggregation of human sin would bring about, and He did something to bring us relief and salvation.

Holy Love - But the love of God is holy love. He had to relieve our sufferings in a holy and righteous way. He could not just sweep our sin under the carpet; He had to make a way consistent with His own nature to relieve us. His answer? Substitution.

Because God is holy, sin must be answered for, the demand that the sinner must die and that wrath be satisfied against all transgression, iniquity and sin. Jesus is the offering God made to Himself , for us.

Compassionate Love - The love of God compelled Him to save us by entering fully into our humanity. God Himself would *feel what we feel,* fully experiencing everything of humanity, (except sin).

God was in Jesus Christ, coming to us, tasting death in all of its forms; hatred and rejection, hunger, thirst, limitation, betrayal, unrequited love, humiliation and even shame. The prophet Isaiah said of Him,

> For he shall grow up before him as a tender plant, and as a root out of a dry ground: he hath no form nor comeliness; and when we shall see him, there is no beauty that we should desire him. He is despised and rejected of men; a man of sorrows, and acquainted with grief: and we hid as it were our faces from him; he was despised, and we esteemed him not. Surely he hath borne our grief, and carried our sorrows: yet we did esteem him stricken, smitten of God, and afflicted. But he was wounded for our transgressions, he was bruised for our iniquities: the chastisement of our peace was upon him; and with his stripes we are healed. All we like sheep have gone astray; we have turned every one to his own way; and the LORD hath laid on him the iniquity of us all. (Isaiah 53:2-6)

Small wonder Charles Wesley taught us to marvel in song of adoration:

> And can it be that I should gain
> an interest in the Savior's blood?
> Died He for me, who caused His pain—
> For me, who Him to death pursued?

Amazing love! How can it be,
That Thou, my God, shouldst die for me?
Amazing love! How can it be,
That Thou, my God, shouldst die for me?

Chapter Twelve
The Only Begotten Son

> For God so loved the world that He gave his only begotten Son, that whosoever believes on Him might not perish but have everlasting life. (John 3:16)

The gift of God, which is eternal life, or being "*born from above*" has been made possible because the righteous and holy God made a righteous way to redeem us sinners. That way involved offering up His "only begotten Son" as a propitiation (sin offering) for us.

What is meant by the mysterious term, "*only begotten Son*"? This is how Jesus describes Himself in John 3:16. We are delving here into the mysteries of the Godhead, so we must tread reverently, and assume at the outset that we could never fully understand Jesus. We can only humbly receive God's self-revelation, to the extent that we are able.

Jesus himself said as much when He proclaimed:

> . . . no man knoweth the Son, but the Father; neither knoweth any man the Father, save the Son, and he to whomsoever the Son will reveal him. (Matthew 11:27)

Only God the Father can fully understand Jesus and only Jesus can fully understand the Father. For us there is only partial (but adequate) revelation of the Father and the Son.

Perhaps we should begin by saying what Jesus is not saying, when he refers to Himself as "the only begotten Son" of the Father.

He is not saying that there was ever a time when He didn't exist. Jesus didn't originate in Bethlehem. He came into the world there, but Jesus is from everlasting, as Micah announced,

> But thou, Bethlehem Ephratah, though thou be little among the thousands of Judah, yet out of thee shall he come forth unto me that is to be ruler in Israel; whose goings forth have been from of old, from everlasting. (Micah 5:2)

Isaiah echoes this in a familiar passage.

> For unto us a child is born, unto us a son is given: and the government shall be upon his shoulder: and his name shall be called Wonderful, Counselor, The mighty God, The everlasting Father, The Prince of Peace. (Isaiah 9:6)

This is not a reference to Jesus' human mother. The apostle John says of Him, "No man hath seen God at any time, the only begotten Son, which is in the bosom of the Father, he hath declared him." (John 1:18)

The "*only begotten Son*" is an eternal term, it refers to "*He who was in the Bosom of the Father*", but who came to reveal God to us. The Son of God is eternal, long before there was a nativity at Bethlehem, He existed as this Proverb affirms.

> Who hath ascended up into heaven, or descended? Who hath gathered the wind in his fists? who hath bound the waters in a garment? who hath established all the ends of the earth? what is his name, and what is his son's name, if thou canst tell? (Proverbs 30:4)

We are definitely not saying that Jesus was created. The Son of God is the creator of all things, as well as the sustainer. He is called "the firstborn of creation" in Colossians 1, but that is a reference to the fact that the new creation, began at the resurrection of Jesus. It is also a reference to the pre-eminence of Jesus in creation. "Who is the image of the invisible God, the firstborn of every creature?"

> For by him were all things created, that are in heaven, and that are in earth, visible and invisible, whether they be thrones, or dominions, or principalities, or powers: all things were created by him, and for him: And he is before all things, and by him all things consist. (Colossians 1:15-18)

The phrase "*only begotten Son*" is a translation of a Greek word in the text, *monogenes*. Jesus is the one and only unique Son of God.

You and I by *new birth* are accepted into the familial fellowship of God. We get to be "sons of God" by adoption, and impartation of eternal life.

Mankind derives its concept of fatherhood and sonship from the ultimate and eternal Father and Son within the Godhead. No matter how warped and misrepresented it can be in this sinful world, true filial devotion, and paternal love come from the Godhead.

Jesus alone is the *monogenes*, the only unique Son of the Father. He is the eternal Son of God, who from of old was in communion with the Father and the Spirit. Thus, Jesus is truly unique. There is no other person like Him and there never can be.

The Son of God from eternity, existed in love, communion and subordination to the Father. He was sent by the Father to this earth, to become a man, that He might enter into our lot, and suffer and die for us as a substitute.

It boggles the mind, that for sinners, rebels and the ruined, warped, perverse race of men, God would send who? His only begotten Son! This is what it took to rescue us, and to bring about a "new birth" for fallen men.

Behold the love of Jesus for the Father!

> Then said Jesus unto them, When ye have lifted up the Son of man, then shall ye know that I am he, and that I do nothing of myself; but as my Father hath taught me, I speak these things. And he that sent me is with me: the Father hath not left me alone; for I do always those things that please him. (John 8:28-29)

Behold also, the love of the Father for the Son. "This is my beloved Son and in Him I am well pleased . . ."

That the eternal Father would send the blessed and

eternal Son, from heaven, to save us from our sins . . . and that the ever-obedient Son, would subordinate Himself to the point of death and shame for us, to do the will of His Father, such mysteries are incomprehensible!

> And we have seen and do testify that the Father sent the Son to be the Saviour of the world. Whosoever shall confess that Jesus is the Son of God, God dwelleth in him, and he in God. And we have known and believed the love that God hath to us. God is love; and he that dwelleth in love dwelleth in God, and God in him. (1 John 4:14-16)

Amazing love how can it be? Behold the love of Father and the Son, for a lost, rebellious, ungrateful and estranged world!

> For God so loved the World that He gave His Only Begotten Son . . . (John 3:16)

Chapter Thirteen
Whosoever (continually) Believes on Him

> For God so loved the world that He gave his only begotten Son, that whosoever believes on Him might not perish but have everlasting life. (John 3:16)

The third chapter of John allows us to overhear a conversation between Nicodemus, the chief rabbi of Israel, and Jesus of Nazareth. Jesus was not trained in the recognized rabbinic schools, but He was approved of God by signs and wonders as well as by the irrefutable doctrine He taught. Nicodemus came to Him, and spoke for other leading rabbis when he acknowledged that Jesus had come from God.

The topic? The New Birth, as the entry into the long-awaited Kingdom of God. Here at this point in the discussion, at John 3:16, Jesus is teaching Nicodemus, (and us) how it is that God could righteously give we sinners a new birth.

God so loved the world that He gave His monogenes. His only unique Son, as a sin offering. God made a righteous way to grant new life to unrighteous men and women, Jesus paid the price for us.

John 3:16 is a much beloved verse of the Bible, perhaps the single most translated prose ever written. But its very familiarity sometimes has the effect on people that they assume that they already *know* it. But the Bible is alive and there is always more light, and helpful enrichment in every verse of scripture.

For example, consider the phrase "whosoever believes in Him". As in the story of the brass serpent lifted up on the pole, anyone who looks up in faith to the "only begotten Son" hanging on the tree will not perish but have everlasting life, (be born again).

Salvation is not just for a particular group, but Jesus died for all. Anyone who hears the gospel and looks believingly unto Jesus shall receive the gift of the new birth, which is also called eternal life.

David Pawson, the man I mentioned earlier who wrote an insightful book about John 3:16[4] makes the point that the word *believes* is in the present continuous tense. The Greek language has more tenses than the English language. (I am no Greek scholar, mind you, but I can read the work of others).

The present continuous tense doesn't often translate into the English, because we don't have one. For example, in Jesus' teaching on prayer, Luke 11:9-10 quotes Him as saying:

> And I say unto you, Ask, and it shall be given you; seek,

---

4 David Pawson, *Is John 3:16 the Gospel?* Terra Nova publications.

> and ye shall find; knock, and it shall be opened unto you. For every one that asketh receiveth; and he that seeketh findeth; and to him that knocketh it shall be opened. (Luke 11:9-10)

Those verbs are also in the present continuous tense, they literally say, "Ask and keep on asking, seek and keep on finding, knock and keep on knocking, for everyone who asks and keeps on asking receives . . ." Knowing the Greek tense clears up a lot of misunderstandings in scripture. Another example is from 1 John 2:15, which says,

> Love not the World nor the things of the world, if any man love the world, the love of the Father is not in him . . ."

Because the word love (agape) is in the present continuous tense, it could just as easily read, *"Don't go on loving the world, nor go on loving the things of the world . . ."*

~~~~~

Anyone who hears the gospel and looks believingly unto Jesus shall receive the gift of the new birth

~~~~~

Going back to our text in John 3:16, we see that the word *believes*, is also in the present continuous tense. It could just as well be understood to say,

> For God so loved the world, that He gave his only begotten Son, so that whosoever **goes on believing** in Him, might not perish but have everlasting life.

Interestingly, Pawson points out that the love God loved the world with, is in the aorist tense, which means that He did it once–*For God (once) thus loved the world.*

When did God love the world? When Jesus died on the cross. The act of God in love for this fallen rebellious world is a once and for all event, it will never be repeated, nor would it ever have to. God loved the world once, and for all time, in the offering of the cross.

God doesn't have a broad and ongoing relationship with the world, approving of this *good* aspect, but disapproving of that *bad* one, yet ever hoping for improvement.

The Holy God has announced that as of the cross, the world is under judgment, the sentence is passed and His attitude towards it is utterly unrelenting, the world is doomed.

> Now is the judgment of this world: now shall the prince of this world be cast out. And I, if I be lifted up from the earth, will draw all men unto me. (John 12:31-32)

But "once" and with perfect and ongoing effect, God loved the world . . . by giving sinful men a way out of their dilemma, through the cross of Jesus.

Back to the text again, Pawson pointed out that the word *believes* is present continuous tense. We are to *go on believing* in Jesus that we might ever have "eternal life".

There are many who are so confused about this that they claim that a person could so backslide that they renounce Jesus entirely and die in their sins, but they suppose that they will be allowed into heaven, because at one point, somewhere along the line, they "believed in Jesus unto salvation".

This false doctrine flies in the face of much of scripture however, for example;

> And you, that were sometime alienated and enemies in your mind by wicked works, yet now hath he reconciled In the body of his flesh through death, to present you holy and unblameable and unreproveable in his sight: **If ye continue in the faith grounded and settled**, and be not moved away from the hope of the gospel, which ye have heard, and which was preached to every creature which is under heaven; whereof I Paul am made a minister. (Colossians 1:21-23)

> Moreover, brethren, I declare unto you the gospel which I preached unto you, which also ye have received, and wherein ye stand; By which also ye are saved, if ye keep in memory what I preached unto you, unless ye have believed in vain. (1 Corinthians 15:1-2)

True, all that Jesus requires of those of us who come to Him for salvation, is that we believe in Him, remaining in faith in His work on the cross and as our High Priest.

But faith isn't static, it is an ongoing dependency, an *abiding* in Jesus, a constant feeding on His finished work, His person, eating and drinking His words. This is the only true *personal relationship* with God.

> I am the true vine, and my Father is the husbandman. Every branch in me that beareth not fruit he taketh away:

and every branch that beareth fruit, he purgeth it, that it may bring forth more fruit. Now ye are clean through the word which I have spoken unto you. Abide in me, and I in you. As the branch cannot bear fruit of itself, except it abide in the vine; no more can ye, except ye abide in me. (John 15:1-4)

Chapter Fourteen
Shall Not Perish?

> For God so loved the world that He gave his only begotten Son, that whosoever believes on Him might not perish but have everlasting life. (John 3:16)

Jesus said that the reason that God, the Father, sent His only begotten Son, (the monogenes) , is that we "might not perish, but have everlasting life."

As we pointed out earlier, the sheer familiarity of John 3:16 often blurs its true power and potency. Children are rightly taught to recite it in Sunday school, much like they are taught the Lord's Prayer, or the Apostles Creed, in an almost rote fashion.

That is why it is beneficial to prayerfully re-approach such familiar passages, examining them word by word and concept by concept with as little preconception as possible.

What does it mean in scripture to perish? We see the word *perish* in other scriptures as well, and fear that the significance of it is vastly unappreciated.

> For the preaching of the cross is to them that perish foolishness; but unto us which are saved it is the power of God." (1 Corinthians 1:18)

> I tell you, Nay: but, except ye repent, ye shall all likewise perish. (Luke 13:5)

> The Lord is not slack concerning his promise, as some men count slackness; but is longsuffering to us-ward, not willing that any should perish, but that all should come to repentance. (2 Peter 3:9)

The Greek word is *Apollumi*, which means to be destroyed, or ruined for an intended use– for example, what we were created for. God doesn't want us to be destroyed, He wants us instead to repent. It can also mean to be lost, to be rendered inoperable, useless, or ruined.

People were created by God for both a general and a specific purpose. Generally it is safe to say that all of us were created that we might know, worship and enjoy communion with our Creator. This is the most important issue of anyone's life.

Specifically, God has given each person unique gifts, desires and talents to glorify Him and to serve others. To fall short of the realization of this, or be indifferent to it is to consign yourself to unfulfillment and frustration. We were made for something specific, "good works which God has ordained for us to walk in".

But sin has started a process of destruction within all of us. In truth everyone in the world is already perishing, outside of Christ. Sin is constantly, steadily, corrupting and eroding our souls.

God estrangement exacts a toll year after year, the process is described several places in scripture, such as in Psalm 1:1–

> Blessed is the man Who walks not in the counsel of the ungodly, Nor stands in the path of sinners, Nor sits in the seat of the scornful.

The truly blessed man avoids the deterioration experienced by sin, through the intervention of God. But the Psalmist pictures the life of the ungodly individual as going from walking, to standing, and finally, to sitting.

As he advances in life, the godless man increasingly becomes set into a fixed moral and spiritual stance; first he is walking, that is he is yet mobile and directable. Eventually he his walk hardens into a stance, he is set in his (errant) way, until finally, as if to illustrate the increasing paralysis of sin, he is seated.

No wonder God admonishes us to "seek the Lord early" in life, while we are still mobile and can change our mind and direction, which is the meaning of repentance. Otherwise, life is a steady downward progression.

Physical death itself doesn't end the destruction. The perishing goes on forever! The soul never stops deteriorating; even in damnation it is eternally ruined. This is the horrifying revelation, that whatever you are in this life, you go on becoming forever. No one remains the same, for we are all in transition.

Perishing is not only a process, brought about by sin, but it is a just punishment from the Holy God.

God must punish all that is evil, sinful, and rebellious. His nature demands it. There must be a "day of wrath" and there will be. Ray Stedman illustrates the dilemma:

> All through the Bible we see God's love is manifest to men and women everywhere in urging them to escape this judgment. God in love pleads with people, "Do not go on to this end!" But ultimately he must judge those who refuse his offer of grace. He says, in effect, "I love you and I can provide all you need. Therefore love me, and you will find the fulfillment your heart is looking for."
>
> But many men and women say, "No, I do not want that. I will take your gifts, I will take all the good things you provide, but I do not want you! Let me run my own life. Let me serve my own ends. Let me have my own kingdom."
>
> To such, God ultimately says, "All right, have it your way!" God has three choices: first, he can let rebellion go on forever and never judge it. In that case the terrible things that are happening on earth, all these distressing injustices, the cruelty, the anger, the hate, the malice, the sorrow, the hurt, the pain, the death that now prevails, must go on forever.[5]

God is not willing that any should perish, but that all should come to repentance. On the other hand, He is willing to punish all sin. He has made a way for men, in the love revealed at Calvary, but He must be true to His righteousness.

5 http://ldolphin.org/hell.html

> Seeing it is a righteous thing with God to recompense tribulation to them that trouble you; And to you who are troubled rest with us, when the Lord Jesus shall be revealed from heaven with his mighty angels, In flaming fire taking vengeance on them that know not God, and that obey not the gospel of our Lord Jesus Christ: Who shall be punished with everlasting destruction from the presence of the Lord, and from the glory of his power. (2 Thessalonians 1:6-9)

> And these shall go away into everlasting punishment: but the righteous into life eternal. (Matthew 25:46)

Perishing is forever; the breakdown and ruin never ends. Jesus tells us that all of the remorse, and regret, "the worm" that gnaws at the eternally awakened conscience, the insatiable "fire" that consumes the soul, is "everlasting".

> And if thine eye offend thee, pluck it out: it is better for thee to enter into the kingdom of God with one eye, than having two eyes to be cast into hell fire: Where their worm dieth not, and the fire is not quenched. (Mark 9:47-48)

The book of Revelation calls it the second death.

> He that hath an ear, let him hear what the Spirit saith unto the churches; He that overcometh shall not be hurt of the second death. (Revelation 2:14)

> Blessed and holy is he that hath part in the first resurrection: on such the second death hath no power, but they shall be priests of God and of Christ, and shall reign with him a thousand years. (Revelation 20:6)

> And the sea gave up the dead which were in it; and death and hell delivered up the dead which were in them: and they were judged every man according to their works. And death and hell were cast into the lake of fire. This is the second death. And whosoever was not found written in the book of life was cast into the lake of fire. (Revelation 20:13-15)

The new birth that Jesus offers, interrupts the process of destruction, it reverses the disintegration of the soul, by the impartation of eternal life, which is the gift of the very life of God. Remember that the discussion of John 3 is the new birth, being "born from above". If there is both a physical and spiritual birth, does it not follow that there is a physical and spiritual death?

As the slogan I once saw put it so well– If you are only born once, you are going to die twice, but if you are born twice, you will only die once!

Flee the wrath of God! Seek Him before it is too late!

Chapter Fifteen
Eternal Life

> For God so loved the world that He gave his only begotten Son, that whosoever believes on Him might not perish but have everlasting life. (John 3:16)

The discussion between Jesus and Nicodemus in John 3, was about the need and the Divine basis for a new birth. The *new birth* is a work of the Holy Spirit of God, man cannot make it happen. Being "born from above" would be the fulfillment of the promise given to Israel that God would give them a "new heart" having taken out of them the "heart of stone", and putting his Spirit within them as individuals.

How could a righteous and holy God do this for such sinners, (as Israel and all of humanity)?

He would send His "only begotten Son" to die as an offering for our sins. This is the basis for the new birth. We don't have to perish, that is, to be ruined forever. We can live, if we accept the gift of God. The gift of God is nothing less than a divine impartation of *eternal life*.

This heavenly gift, which speaks to our deepest need, is much misunderstood even by many Christians. Salvation is a multi-faceted subject, for the fall of man from God has ruined us on every level.

Our deepest need is for life from God, for our problem is that in our sins, we are dead to God. We were created to worship Him, to lovingly respond to His will, to feed off of His Word, to enjoy God and walk with Him through life.

> But we are all "dead in trespasses and sins . . ."
>
> This I say therefore, and testify in the Lord, that ye henceforth walk not as other Gentiles walk, in the vanity of their mind, Having the understanding darkened, being alienated from the life of God through the ignorance that is in them, because of the blindness of their heart: Who being past feeling have given themselves over unto lasciviousness, to work all uncleanness with greediness. (Ephesians 4:17-19)

Eternal life is God's answer to man's spiritual death. In Jesus, the dead live again, we come alive to God.

The lost capacity to know Him, worship and love Him, to respond to Him is restored to the believer in Jesus. A Christian conversion is nothing less than a resurrection from the dead. Jesus alone can call the dead from their graves and grant them eternal life!

> Verily, verily, I say unto you, He that heareth my word, and believeth on him that sent me, hath everlasting life, and shall not come into condemnation; but is passed from

> death unto life. Verily, verily, I say unto you, The hour is coming, and now is, when the dead shall hear the voice of the Son of God: and they that hear shall live. (John 5:24-25)

> The wages of sin is death, but the gift of God is eternal life through Jesus Christ our Lord. (Romans 6:23)

What is Eternal Life?

Eternal life is a quality of life – The point of the term "eternal life" is not that we live forever, for all of humanity will be around forever; conscious, self-aware, with memory, whether saint or sinner. Jesus tells us that at His command, there will be both a resurrection unto life and a resurrection of damnation.

> Marvel not at this: for the hour is coming, in the which all that are in the graves shall hear his voice, And shall come forth; they that have done good, unto the resurrection of life; and they that have done evil, unto the resurrection of damnation. (John 5:28-29)

The point of the phrase "eternal life" is that the life comes from eternity. It is a reference to quality of life, not a quantity. This is the life of God, given to us through the Son of God. We become "*partakers of the Divine nature*" through the knowledge of Jesus our Lord and Savior.

Eternal life starts now–I have met people whose hope

is that when they die they will receive eternal life. But if you wait until then, it will be too late! Eternal life begins the moment one is born again by accepting Jesus, (John 1:1213), believing in His name, that is, the things He is and stands for and has accomplished.

> But these are written, that ye might believe that Jesus is the Christ, the Son of God; and that believing ye might have life through his name. (John 20:31)

Eternal life is dependant life – The analogy Jesus used to describe the believer's reception of eternal life as the gift of God, comes from the vineyard. He is the "true vine" and we who believe are the branches. Eternal life is communicated unto us as we "abide in Jesus", the source of eternal life.

Eternal life is knowing "*the only true God and Jesus Christ*" (John 17:3) whom He sent. It is not a separate and static gift, but an ongoing reliance on and steady communion with Jesus.

> If any man remain in me he shall bring forth much fruit . . .

We can know that we have eternal life– The first epistle of John was written that we might know that we have eternal life . . . (1 John 5:13).

But 1 John 5:13 is not just a proof text, He speaks of "these things" by which we can have assurance. The things He speaks of in the letter are the tests of eternal life, based on three propositional statements about the nature of the God who gives us a share in His life.

"God is light . . ." (1 John 1:5) – The test here is, that since God is light, then those who have received the life of God are willing to live in the light, they confess their sin, in fact they are at war with indwelling sin, for they hate sin.

He that doesn't hate sin, doesn't have eternal life.

"God is love . . ." (1 John 4:8) because God is love, those who have the life of God love one another. "We know we have passed from death to life because we love one another . . ." (1 John 3:14)

> Whosoever hateth his brother is a murderer: and ye know that no murderer hath eternal life abiding in him. (1 John 3:15)

> Jesus Christ has come in the flesh . . . (1 John 4:2)

He that has eternal life, is going to believe the truth about Jesus, His incarnation, His deity, the full doctrine of Christ. Eternal life will always lead you to the true Jesus.

Those who have not eternal life, evidence it by straying away from the doctrine of Christ (2 John 9). They have not been born "of the truth" therefore they have no inward affinity to it.

This is threefold test of eternal life, an ethical test, a test of love, and a test of truth, by which we might know that we have the Son and the life.

Chapter Sixteen
Jesus Wasn't Sent to Condemn the World

> For God sent not his Son into the world to condemn the world; but that the world through him might be saved. He that believeth on him is not condemned: but he that believeth not is condemned already, because he hath not believed in the name of the only begotten Son of God. (John 3:17-18)

We have been looking at the discussion between Jesus and Israel's chief rabbi, Nicodemus, on the subject of entry into the Kingdom of God.

The only possibility of entering the Kingdom of God, according to Jesus, is by the "new birth", i.e. being "born from above".

Man is a sinner indeed and needs forgiveness, but he has a deeper need yet, because he is spiritually dead.

Sinful, fallen, estranged and ruined man can and must be born again! Without a spiritual resurrection, man is dead to God.

He has no capacity to perceive, fellowship, or to receive anything from God. But a man cannot manufacture a "new birth" of his own. It is solely a work of God.

The new birth is the gift of God, performed by the Holy Spirit of God. Sinful man has been qualified for this gift by the sending of the Son of God from heaven, to be the sin offering for us.

> For God so loved the world that He gave His only begotten Son . . .

There is so much rich theology in these spare, simple verses. For example, we can behold the Godhead in this revelation. It was the Father, who sent the Son to be the Savior of the world. Before anything else was, God has always been. One God, but in three persons: Father, Son and Holy Spirit.

The eternal Father sent the eternal Son out of love for the fallen rebellious world. The Son is ever lovingly subordinate to the Father, living to please and honor the Father. The Spirit ever proceeds from the Father and Son, honoring the Son.

> Then answered Jesus and said unto them, Verily, verily, I say unto you, The Son can do nothing of himself, but what he seeth the Father do: for what things soever he doeth, these also doeth the Son likewise. For the Father loveth the Son, and sheweth him all things that himself doeth: and he will shew him greater works than these, that ye may marvel. (John 5:19-20)

That the Son of God was sent into the world, is a profound mystery. We cannot understand it, we can only worshipfully receive the revelation, with lowly awe. From before the world, the Father sent the Son and the Son was ever willing to come . . .

> Wherefore when he cometh into the world, he saith, Sacrifice and offering thou wouldest not, but a body hast thou prepared me: In burnt offerings and sacrifices for sin thou hast had no pleasure. Then said I, Lo, I come (in the volume of the book it is written of me,) to do thy will, O God. (Hebrews 10:5-7)

No one else could say that they "*came into this world*" in any other sense than that they were born here at some point in time.

But the Son was sent here, (from heaven). He who was from of old, whose habitation was in eternity, in constant communion with the Father, the original gardener from Eden, the ultimate Bridegroom, actually entered into this world.

He condescended from an infinite height to come unto us. He came down to us. Why did the Son have to come down? Because we who are fallen are so bankrupt and dead, that there would be no other way for us to ever get up to heaven. The Father sent the Son into the world.

But now we read the motive, as well as the negative of the motive, for here we are told that *the Son was not sent to condemn the world, but to save it.*

Why does He have to tell us that Jesus wasn't sent to condemn the world? Shouldn't that be obvious?

As a matter of fact, Jesus tells us this because it would be easy to think, that indeed Jesus did come to condemn the world. The message Jesus brings to the rebellious, God-hating world, does sound condemning. For example . . .

> For I say unto you, That except your righteousness shall exceed the righteousness of the scribes and Pharisees, ye shall in no case enter into the kingdom of heaven. (Matthew 5:20)

> Enter ye in at the strait gate: for wide is the gate, and broad is the way, that leadeth to destruction, and many there be which go in thereat: Because strait is the gate, and narrow is the way, which leadeth unto life, and few there be that find it. (Matthew 7:13-14)

> There were present at that season some that told him of the Galileans, whose blood Pilate had mingled with their sacrifices. And Jesus answering said unto them, "Suppose ye that these Galileans were sinners above all the Galileans, because they suffered such things? I tell you, Nay: but, except ye repent, ye shall all likewise perish. Or those eighteen, upon whom the tower in Siloam fell, and slew them, think ye that they were sinners above all men that dwelt in Jerusalem? I tell you, Nay: but, except ye repent, ye shall all likewise perish." (Luke 13:1-5)

Jesus spent a lot of time warning sinners about the certainty of judgment, hell, the regret, the agony, "weeping and gnashing of teeth". He also spent much of His ministry and teaching showing men that they are sinners, exposing hypocrisy, teaching the true meaning of the Ten Commandments, convicting men of the danger they are in for breaking them.

I once told a person I was witnessing to, that Jesus

spoke far more about heaven than He did hell. (I was sure I was right, it seemed right that Jesus would always be "positive").

But I had a thought to check my facts out, so I started counting in Matthew, all of the verses which spoke of heaven and comparing those to the number of verses speaking of hell. I quit about halfway through, because it was so lop-sided in favor of hell, I felt foolish!

I see why people could get the impression that Jesus came to condemn the world. When you think about it, much of Jesus preaching is condemning to the world. I am speaking of the real content of the words of Jesus in the Gospels, not the modern *psychological Jesus* or the popular *positive thinking Jesus* or the *new age Jesus* proclaimed by the false prophets of our day.

Look at the words of the real Jesus, and see the penetrating conviction, the utter condemnation of all men, the warnings against self righteousness, and the inadequacy of religious observance.

Actually, it can be quite frightening.

But the Father didn't send the Son to condemn the world; Jesus came to save the world! We would say similarly of a skilled doctor who was a cancer specialist, that he was not trained, educated and hired by a medical center to scare people, although his diagnosis probably does just that. The idea is to heal them.

But first they must know that they are sick and need radical treatment!

The Father loves the world, in spite of its profound sin, its hatred of God, its pride, and arrogance. God loves men, and doesn't want any to perish, but all to come to the saving knowledge of the Son.

To "believe on the name of the Son of God", is nothing less than to believe in Jesus, who He is and what He did for us, to accept Him, and to enter fully into the new birth He offers. This is why Jesus came to us, this is why the Father sent Him.

Chapter Seventeen

Unbelievers Are Already Condemned

> He that believeth on him is not condemned: but he that believeth not is condemned already, because he hath not believed in the name of the only begotten Son of God. And this is the condemnation, that light is come into the world, and men loved darkness rather than light, because their deeds were evil. For every one that doeth evil hateth the light, neither cometh to the light, lest his deeds should be reproved. (John 3:18-20)

In John chapter 3 , Jesus tells us that He didn't come into the world to "condemn the world". He didn't have to, for the world, which rejects the Father and "His only begotten Son" was and is already condemned. All men are continuously condemned by God's law, as well as by their consciences which tell them, that they are not right with God.

All men carry in themselves some sense of a share in the shame and guilt of the human race. This is the reason why religion is an inescapable aspect of life. Condemnation is the inner knowledge of a deep and personal sense of failure to live up to a standard. Much of what are currently considered to be *psychological problems* are outcomes of condemnation.

Men know in their hearts that they don't measure up, that they are sinners. Condemnation lies behind the fear of death also, for there is a universally instinctive knowledge that men have about death. Men know that death isn't really natural, and that it is a punishment that it has to do with judgment.

Men also share universally a sense that there is something exalted about man. Not only do we all share in the shame of Adam, but that we share in the "Image of God" in which we were created.

But this amplifies our condemnation, because we know we are not mere animals, following instinct, but reasoning and responsible moral agents, who must give account of our actions. We have shattered and distorted the "Image of God".

Thus, "he that *believes not is condemned already*". Jesus didn't have to condemn the world, although His coming does intensify the already present condemning effect.

This is because Jesus' coming was and is as a light that reveals everything else in its true light, and causes all that is false to be seen for what it really is.

For example, the *Pharisees* and *Sadducees* pretended to be *holy men of God*, presenting themselves to the people of the land as truly pious, God-fearing worshippers.

But with the coming of Jesus, true holiness and piety was revealed to everybody. In Him, we see what it means to be a *Father pleaser*, a *lover of God*, true devotion to God, and what it really means to believe and follow the law of God. What does it mean to truly fear God? It means nothing less than to live as Jesus lived.

> Again, a new commandment I write unto you, which thing is true in him and in you: because the darkness is past, and the true light now shineth. (1 John 2:8)

The effect of the life of Jesus, then and now, was to cause the fake holiness and piety of Pharisees and Sadducees to be seen for the shallow hypocrisy that it was and is. With the coming of Jesus, religious pretense was no longer possible.

Self deceit, and hypocrisy – i.e. pretending not to be what you are, or pretending to be what you are not – becomes impossible in the light of Jesus.

There can be no neutrality, for Jesus compels a choice. God cannot be known outside of Jesus. There can be no real "holiness" apart from Him. People are compelled to either be for or against Jesus and His word. This is the meaning of the word *crisis*, which is the root of the word for *condemnation*.

Any encounter with Jesus forces a crisis, a watershed moment. The *crisis of this world* was the cross of Jesus. There at the cross, the world was condemned by God. All of its works were judged as worthy of death and destruction, and the proud prince of this world was defeated and slated for his own perdition.

> Now is the judgment of this world: now shall the prince of this world be cast out. And I, if I be lifted up from the earth, will draw all men unto me. (John 12:31-32)

Now is the crisis of this world! The cross is the condemnation of the whole world, the greatest negative ever, because on it, Jesus took upon Himself all of the sins, yea He represented all of the people of the world, and bore us to death and judgment.

The world is already under Divine condemnation, it was judged at the cross of Jesus. The world will not be healed or improved. It will not be made into a better place. God has already pronounced the final sentence on this world. All that awaits is the perdition it deserves.

But in Jesus, for the time being, condemned men and women can "pass out of condemnation" and into "everlasting life".

Chapter Eighteen
The Damned Reject the Light

> He that believeth on him is not condemned: but he that believeth not is condemned already, because he hath not believed in the name of the only begotten Son of God. And this is the condemnation, that light is come into the world, and men loved darkness rather than light, because their deeds were evil. For every one that doeth evil hateth the light, neither cometh to the light, lest his deeds should be reproved. (John 3:18-20)

The new birth that Jesus spoke of in His talk with Nicodemus, is good news. We can start all over again with God. We can become "as children" again. We can be born again unto God, and walk in a new relationship with Him as His children.

Furthermore, we can enter into a hope of eternal glory, the very glory which by the fall of man we have all fallen short of. God the Father has made a way to bring us into the fellowship of His Son.

This was all made possible by the gift of love, that is, the offering of the Son of God for our sins.

All sins can be forgiven, All of the evil things we

have done against God and one another have been accounted for, and paid for in full, in the sacrifice Jesus made on Calvary.

Jesus died for all sins and for every sinner,

> . . . once and for all, the just for the unjust to bring us to God . . .(1 Peter 3:18).

But receiving the gift of the new birth requires that, like the risen Lazarus, we step out of our own tomb of darkness and walk into the light of God .

What does it mean to walk in the Light of Jesus?

> Then spake Jesus again unto them, saying, I am the light of the world: he that followeth me shall not walk in darkness, but shall have the light of life. (John 8:12)

What does light do? Light reveals things, it allows for things to be seen as they truly are. This is the effect of the coming of Jesus–

> The people that walked in darkness have seen a great light: they that dwell in the land of the shadow of death, upon them hath the light shined. (Isaiah 9:2)

Jesus revealed by His words, and His works, "the only true God". Now we know fully what God is like, for in seeing Jesus we have seen the Father. "*The darkness is past and the true light now shineth . . .*" The God Jesus reveals is a loving Father, merciful and gracious, healing, and resurrecting. His words are life, He knows about us, our struggles, fears, and faults.

Jesus also revealed that God is a holy and righteous judge who will one day summon all mankind before His throne of judgment.

Most of what we know biblically of hellfire comes from Jesus. We get expressions such as "*weeping and gnashing of teeth*", and "*outer darkness*" from the words of Jesus! Jesus also reveals the true character of men. By Jesus, the secrets of men's hearts are fully revealed, and it isn't a flattering picture. Men are fallen, blind, hypocritical, and murderous. They are selfish, and unforgiving, and estranged from God by their sins.

Jesus shatters the world's estimation of itself. He contradicts its proud humanism entirely, exposing the utter spiritual and moral bankruptcy of even the *best* of men. He holds back nothing in His critical analysis of the hearts of all men.

> That which cometh out of the man, that defileth the man. For from within, out of the heart of men, proceed evil thoughts, adulteries, fornications, murders, Thefts, covetousness, wickedness, deceit, lasciviousness, an evil eye, blasphemy, pride, foolishness: All these evil things come from within, and defile the man. (Mark 7:20-23)

His cross is perhaps the greatest offense of all, because it presupposes profound human guilt, as well as being a statement of our human inability to atone for ourselves.

The cross is also a profound revelation of the divine hatred of sin. Jesus died for our sins, as a substitute and an offering to God. We look at the tortured figure shuttering on the cross in agony, abandoned by all, even by His God, mocked and humiliated by His enemies, and we breathe a whispered prayer:

> Dear Lord is this what it took to save me from my sins? Is this how bad sin really is? Could the breach between God and man be so great that it took this to bring us to you?

But the wicked are offended by this revelation of Jesus. They take an exception to the exposure of the true nature of man as revealed in Jesus, and especially in His cross. The light is too glaring, the exposure is uncomfortable because it is condemning, even damning.

~~~~~

We can be born again unto God, and walk in a new relationship with Him as His children.

~~~~~

In fact many spend their lives fleeing the light of Jesus, shutting the shades, closing the door, and averting their gaze whenever the light happens to shine. They don't want to be told that man is fallen, and that they need to be rescued from their own sins.

The call to be "born again" is in itself an insult. *Why should I start all over again, I am good enough as I am!* People don't want to be born again if it means confessing their sins to God, or admitting their sinfulness and spiritual bankruptcy.

Remember what Paul the apostle told us by the Holy Spirit in Romans 1. The ungodly are under divine wrath because they "suppress the truth in unrighteousness" They fully know that they were created by a personal God, that they have broken or failed to live up to any moral code, and furthermore, that because of this, they are liable to judgment.

> And even as they did not like to retain God in their knowledge, God gave them over to a reprobate mind, to do those things which are not convenient; (Romans 1:28)

Jesus said that the real condemnation of the wicked is that when light came into the world, ". . . *men loved the darkness more than they loved the light* . . ." They actually love to not know the truth about themselves, they do not want to be seen by God, nor are they willing to be known for who they really are. They refuse to see themselves in the light of God.

This is a truly deep look into the psychology of godless man, that he prefers fantasy and illusion to truth, for the truth humbles him. It shows him to be a dependent and needy creature. He doesn't want to face a judge, so he imagines there isn't an ultimate one. Man wants to craft his own rules, his own personal ethic, therefore he resents and even hates the commandments of God.

He would create his own world, on his own terms, and define his own righteousness, if only it were possible. He doesn't want to know the *right way*. Man crafts his own plan of salvation, but always one that exalts man, never one that humbles him. Fallen man hates the light of Jesus.

Jesus warns us that this will be the basis for the final

judgment, the love or hatred, acceptance or rejection of the light that came into the world.

Chapter Nineteen
Doing the Truth

> And this is the condemnation, that light is come into the world, and men loved darkness rather than light, because their deeds were evil. For every one that doeth evil hateth the light, neither cometh to the light, lest his deeds should be reproved. But he that doeth truth cometh to the light, that his deeds may be made manifest, that they are wrought in God. (John 3:19-21)

Jesus' discussion with Nicodemus, that there is a "new birth" ended on the related topic of the final judgment of all men at the throne of God. Being "born from above" is the only way possible for men to escape the condemnation that they are already under, as well as the ultimate and final damnation we all deserve. All men are sinners and liable to judgment.

Why will so many be condemned forever, to spend eternity being ruined and estranged from all of the comforts and beauty that God has prepared for man?

Jesus, the one to whom God the Father has committed all judgment, condenses the issue down to one charge. The Judgment comes because when the light came to us from God, men preferred darkness instead, rejecting Jesus, and all that He did and stood for.

They don't accept His revelation of man's heart, and of man's need, and most of all they abhor the message of the Cross and all that it implies.

This is the very meaning of evil. Not so much the magnitude of harmful works or words. Nor is evil defined by the extent of the damage done by our sins. Rather, evil as defined by Jesus, is the adamant refusal of God's light, the willful shutting out of the heart God's truth.

Evil is the preference towards darkness over light, the opting for lies, fantasies, and self-serving illusions rather than for divine truth, as revealed particularly in Jesus.

What does the gospel mean by the expression *the truth*?

Truth is not a general word, as we now use it, such as the truth of algebra, physics, history, geometry, and so on. When the apostles spoke of the truth, they were referring to "The Truth" as the only genuine revelation of spiritual reality.

For example, truth is the revelation of who God is, who and what man is, the plight of man, and the God appointed answer to our dilemma, and the nature of sin and redemption.

Truth is the eternal reality as revealed by Jesus, who said of Himself, "*I am the truth*".

How could we know these things other than by revelation? God has so created the world, that He has made it possible for men to discover physical realities, such as the laws of chemistry, geometry and mathematics. But science can't be the answer to every question.

The answers to questions such as *Who am I? Why was I created? Why is there evil and suffering?*, require divine revelation.

Only the Creator can give us those answers. The Lord Jesus is the fullest revelation of the invisible God. He is the truth. God raised Him from the dead to certify Him to us, that He truly died for our sins as a divinely appointed substitute. His evaluation of the human condition is the truth.

Likewise His work to remedy it, and His promises and warning to those who accept or reject Him, this is what is meant as *the truth*.

Doing truth means fully accepting Jesus' revelation and acting upon it. "*He that doeth truth comes to the light* . . .", that is, he takes Jesus seriously, admits that He is right, and is willing to see himself and have others see him, as God sees him. No more pretense, no more hiding or play acting, simply accepting the implication of the cross, that *I am a sinner, for whom Jesus died.*

> But he that doeth truth cometh to the light, that his deeds may be made manifest, that they are wrought in God. (John 3:21)

It is living with the acceptance that everything I do or have done has been "in the sight of God" anyway, so I may as well be real about it. God sees me, and I am glad of it! He sees all of me, *the good, the bad and the ugly*, but He made provision for me on Calvary, because I need it! Hypocrisy is shortsighted because sooner or later all is coming out into the open.

Doing truth involves confessing our sins, justifying God, and being willing to live in the light of God's exposure. It is dropping the fig leaves of a contrived self righteousness, and allowing Jesus' blood to wash away our sins. It is the willingness to live our lives openly in the community of truth, among the body of Christ who love the truth also.

> But if we walk in the light, as he is in the light, we have fellowship one with another, and the blood of Jesus Christ his Son cleanseth us from all sin. If we say that we have no sin, we deceive ourselves, and the truth is not in us. If we confess our sins, he is faithful and just to forgive us our sins, and to cleanse us from all unrighteousness. If we say that we have not sinned, we make him a liar, and his word is not in us. (1 John 1:7-10)

Paul would echo Jesus, in 2 Thessalonians 2 when he warned of those who,

> . . . with all deceivableness of unrighteousness in them that perish; because they received not the love of the truth, that they might be saved. And for this cause God shall send them strong delusion, that they should believe a lie: That they all might be damned who believed not the truth, but had pleasure in unrighteousness. (2 Thessalonians 2:10-12)

It comes down to what people love and hate doesn't it?

We are warned that there are only two categories of people. Those who "love the darkness", who actually fancy the lies, the obfuscation, the cloud of denial that they are sinners before their Creator, in danger of judgment, and in need of redemption. They gravitate to any theory or religious system that allows them to evade the truth.

The ones who love the darkness simply have to believe the lie. It is what they resonate with, it is in them, and therefore they gravitate towards it.

If there wasn't a Benny Hinn or a Ken Copeland or the other heretics plaguing the church, someone would have to invent them, because the constituency for them is already there. They love the lie, therefore they will have the lie, sooner or later.

There are also those who "*receive the love of the truth*". They love the church or preacher who shows them their sins, they admit the claims of the gospel, that we are all sinners, in need of forgiveness and justification.

Through the new birth, and the gospel, the *truth* has transformed them, it resonates with them. They have been born again of it, therefore they have an inward affinity to the *truth*, feeding their souls with it, living in it, promoting it at any cost. Jesus said,

> . . . All who are of the truth shall hear my voice . . . (John 18:37).

Are you "of the truth"?

Chapter Twenty

He Must Increase, I Must Decrease

> John answered and said, A man can receive nothing, except it be given him from heaven. Ye yourselves bear me witness, that I said, I am not the Christ, but that I am sent before him. He that hath the bride is the bridegroom: but the friend of the bridegroom, which standeth and heareth him, rejoiceth greatly because of the bridegroom's voice: this my joy therefore is fulfilled. He must increase, but I must decrease. (John 3:27-30)

The Gospel of John chapter 3 is constructed in such a way as to make a specific theological point. There is a continuity of thought, from Jesus' discussion with Nicodemus, to the testimony of John the Baptist.

It is written, that, "By the mouth of two or three witnesses everything shall be confirmed". This additional vignette of John the Baptist's words to his disciples serves to reinforce the main points of Jesus and Nicodemus' discussion. The background is the concern John's disciples had, when they perceived that Jesus' ministry was eclipsing John's in scope and influence.

> And they came unto John, and said unto him, Rabbi, he that was with thee beyond Jordan, to whom thou barest witness, behold, the same baptizeth, and all men come to him. (John 3:26)

The attitude John displays in response to this concern of his disciples, about his *ministry*, is not only a correct and God-centered personal response, but it serves as a model, to the broader spiritual posture we all must assume, in order to enter into the new birth.

John the Baptist, of whom Jesus said,

> Verily I say unto you, among them that are born of women there hath not risen a greater than John the Baptist . . .

is going to show us the way to look at ourselves and most importantly, how to look at Jesus. He models to us the very attitudes that one must have to be born again. Let us receive his words of wisdom–

> A man can receive nothing, except it be given him from heaven. (John 3:27)

In the immediate context, John is responding to the fear of his disciples that Jesus' ministry of preaching repentance is overshadowing their own. John's answer goes far beyond that however. All that really matters to any of us, is what God has given to us.

God's grace is what matters, not works. The gift of God shall last, not human accomplishment. Spiritually speaking, whatever it is that any of us has accumulated through our own efforts, amounts to nothing. Only what God gives is of consequence.

Back to the original context, John is assuring his disciples, "God is giving those crowds to Jesus, even as just as for a brief moment, God gave us those crowds who thronged to my preaching." Even so in the bigger picture, the only real issue of eternal consequence is, "Have you been given to Jesus?"

Jesus would soon tell a crowd of followers on the verge of abandoning Him the same thing, saying:

> All that the Father giveth me shall come to me; and him that cometh to me I will in no wise cast out. For I came down from heaven, not to do mine own will, but the will of him that sent me. And this is the Father's will which hath sent me, that of all which he hath given me I should lose nothing, but should raise it up again at the last day. (John 6:37-39)

Confidence in the sovereignty of God, is what is being expressed here. God is the determining factor in the new birth, yea in all things. A man has nothing except what God gives him. Jesus would say something similar in His trial before Pilate, who was astonished that Jesus didn't beg for His own life before him–

> And went again into the judgment hall, and saith unto Jesus, "Whence art thou?" But Jesus gave him no answer. Then saith Pilate unto him, "speakest thou not unto me? Knowest thou not that I have power to crucify thee, and have power to release thee?" Jesus answered, "Thou couldest have no power at all against me, except it were given thee from above: therefore he that delivered me unto thee hath the greater sin." (John 19:9-11)

> He that hath the bride is the bridegroom: but the friend of the bridegroom, which standeth and heareth him, rejoiceth greatly because of the bridegroom's voice: this my joy therefore is fulfilled. (John 3:29)

What is the point of the best man at a wedding? Is the best man the one everyone is waiting for? Is he the man of the hour? Of course not. The best man is the friend of the bridegroom, the one designated to make the preparations for the wedding, to gather the people together, make sure the bride has everything she needs to be prepared for the wedding.

Once the groom enters the room, the best man recedes into the background. He knows he has done his part, and that it's not about him; it is about the groom! He is happy for the attention that the groom receives. So it is with those of us who witness for Jesus. Salvation isn't about us; everything is about Jesus. The church isn't an end in itself; it is a means to a greater end, for the Bridegroom comes!

> He must increase, but I must decrease. (John 3:30)

The Bible begins with a wedding and ends with a wedding. At the first wedding, Adam, a man with a scar in his side is presented a bride, (the scar was because part of his side had been taken out by God, to prepare the bride).

The first groom utters a prophecy, "for this cause shall a man leave his father and mother and shall cleave to his wife and they two shall be one flesh."

At the last wedding, which is the ultimate one, the "*marriage supper of the Lamb*", Jesus, the groom, also has a scar in His side, as well as in His hands, for He has been pierced and was crucified to purchase His bride. His bride, the church is being prepared even now.

Marriage is not for the selfish. The bride cannot be a *feminist*, in the sense of modern feminism, unwilling to let go of SELF, nor to take on the new name, holding on to her own *personhood*, identity and career. She must let go of her own life, and be willing to take on the life of the groom.

The new birth teaches us that self must no longer be all important; self-righteousness, self ambition, self-esteem, self-identity, self discovery, self-expression, self-realization and so on. All of the things that our toxic culture is telling us is so important, the new birth flies in the face of. One cannot have it unless they are to the point of self-renunciation.

John the Baptist is talking about far more than a ministerial comparison. He is giving us the mindset required of one in order to receive the new birth. Jesus must increase. His thinking, His words, His works, His outlook, is what counts, not my own. His righteousness alone pleases the Father, He alone is worthy of all of my affection, praise, pursuit. Jesus must increase indeed!

These are the attitudes, and the outlook of those who would receive the heavenly gift of the birth from above.

Chapter Twenty-one
The Person of Christ

> He that cometh from above is above all: he that is of the earth is earthly, and speaketh of the earth: he that cometh from heaven is above all. And what he hath seen and heard, that he testifieth; and no man receiveth his testimony. He that hath received his testimony hath set to his seal that God is true. For he whom God hath sent speaketh the words of God: for God giveth not the Spirit by measure unto him. The Father loveth the Son, and hath given all things into his hand. (John 3:31-35)

The new birth is all about Jesus. It was the offering of His life which made it possible for a Holy God to offer sinners a new heart and

> a washing of regeneration and renewal in the Holy Spirit. (Titus 3:5)

In Jesus we are "*born again unto a living hope . . .*", but "*Not of corruptible seed but incorruptible, by the Word of God . . .*" (1 Peter 1:3 and 1:23).

The new birth was given by God to us that we might

enter a process whereby we are steadily "*. . . conformed to the Image of the Son of God*" (Romans 8:29).

The goal is that we share in the nature and character of Jesus. Birth from above is entered into by those who "*receive Him . . .*", they are the ones who by faith become "sons of God", that is, those who receive the Messiah Jesus, as the Lord and Savior and sacrifice for sin.

> But as many as received him, to them gave he power to become the sons of God, even to them that believe on his name: Which were born, not of blood, nor of the will of the flesh, nor of the will of man, but of God. (John 1:12-13)

Jesus is the author and source and cause of the new birth, having been sent by God the Father, that we might have the indescribable privilege of being begotten of God.

Therefore it is fitting that John the evangelist was led by the Holy Spirit to conclude this chapter of his gospel on the new birth, with this testimony to Jesus by John the Baptist. It was in response to a question that was asked of John's disciples about *purification.*

Judaism already had *baptisms* and various ceremonial washings for ritual uncleanness before John the Baptist. But the faithful Jews in that day could accept that John's baptism was a valid reform movement within Judaism, in the tradition of Elijah or the other prophets. A first century believing Jew could conclude that obviously God had raised up John, to call His people back to Him in repentance.

But with the emergence of Jesus, they perceived something further. John was already telling people to quit following him, that they might follow Jesus. Why should they who responded to John's call to repentance, now concern themselves with this new movement which had subsequently arisen?

Who is this Jesus, who supersedes rabbinic Judaism and even its reform, through the God appointed prophet, John (Baptist)? John answers in these succinct Christological statements on the person of Christ.

> He that cometh from above is above all: he that is of the earth is earthly, and speaketh of the earth: he that cometh from heaven is above all. (John 3:31)

Jesus didn't come from Bethlehem, though He was born there. As the prophet Micah tells us,

> But thou, Bethlehem Ephratah, though thou be little among the thousands of Judah, yet out of thee shall he come forth unto me that is to be ruler in Israel; whose goings forth have been from of old, from everlasting. (Micah 5:2)

Jesus is no reformer, nor is He merely a prophet, or a servant of God. When we are dealing with Jesus, we are dealing with "*the Son of Man, who came down from heaven . . .*" (see John 3:13), who is God incarnate!

He that is of the earth is earthly and speaks of the earth– refers to all other men. Even the greatest prophets lived and operated out of a human perspective, other than the times when they were used by God to convey

His holy word. Being of the earth means being human, limited, and having a temporal frame of reference.

Jesus is the man who is the "*. . . Lord from heaven . . .*" (1 Corinthians 15:47).

Jesus comes speaking as an eyewitness to eternal things –"*And what he hath seen and heard, that he testifieth; and no man receiveth his testimony . . .*"

Earlier in the chapter Jesus said something similar to Nicodemus, "*We speak the things we have seen, and you believe not . . .*"

Having come from eternity, Jesus needed no vision or revelation to know the mind of God, as other previous prophets. Jesus is in an entirely different class of being. He was there, when Adam and Eve fell, when Abraham was called, when Satan fell like lightning!

> And he said unto them, "I beheld Satan as lightning fall from heaven . . ." (Luke 10:18)

> Your father Abraham rejoiced to see my day: and he saw it, and was glad." (John 8:56)

What Jesus knows about God, man, eternity, truth, the gap between man and God, salvation, is personal knowledge. He knows it first hand, none of it was mediated to Him.

Why should we believe that? The resurrection compels us to believe in Jesus.

Jesus' testimony is the testimony of God himself. Therefore those who believe in Jesus are saying that *God is right, He is true.* To reject the testimony of Jesus is tantamount to saying that God is a liar! This is what it means to set your seal that God is true. It is as though God put hot wax as a seal on a scroll of His testimony, and you have an embossed signet ring, which you press into the wax, as a way of saying "Amen".

In another place we are given a summary of the testimony of God:

> . . . if we receive the witness of men, the witness of God is greater; For this is the witness of God which he hath testified of his Son. He that believeth on the Son of God hath the witness in himself: he that believeth not God hath made him a liar; because he believeth not the record that God gave of his Son. And this is the record, that God hath given to us eternal life, and this life is in his Son. He that hath the Son hath life; and he that hath not the Son of God hath not life. (1 John 5:9-12)

God gives us eternal life through the Son, Jesus.

He is the one who "*came by water and by blood*", that is, He was always the Christ, before His baptism, and He never stopped being the Christ, even when He was crucified. There was never a time when He became "Christ", for He is the eternal One, who came into the world to save us.

> The Father loveth the Son, and hath given all things into his hand. (John 3:35)

All things have been committed to Him by the Father – salvation, the new birth, final judgment, the Kingdom of God, forgiveness of sins, and life everlasting have all been committed to Jesus by the Father.

God cannot be known other than through Jesus. A person's attitude towards God is revealed by his attitude towards Jesus. Salvation is only possible through Jesus, there is no other name given among men whereby we might be saved, than through Jesus.

One day, every knee will bow, and every tongue confess that Jesus Christ is Lord, to the glory of the Father.

Chapter Twenty-two

The Only Two Outcomes

> He that believeth on the Son hath everlasting life: and he that believeth not the Son shall not see life; but the wrath of God abideth on him. (John 3:36)

The final words in this chapter on the new birth, are given to the one Jesus designated as "greatest man born of a woman", John the Baptist. Jesus had spoken to Nicodemus of the necessity of the new birth, the fact that being "*born from above*" is an act of God, the Holy Spirit.

Jesus also gives the teacher of Israel, (and us) the scriptural warrant for it , for this is the giving of a new tender heart spoken of in the prophet Ezekiel (chapter 36). Our Lord also revealed that the basis for this gift of God's grace to sinners, is nothing less than the sacrificial offering of the "only begotten Son".

But John, the evangelist included as a second witness to the new birth, the testimony of John the Baptist. His emphasis was on the person of Christ Himself. He is the "Son who descended" from heaven to bring bankrupt men this grace. The Father has committed everything, salvation and judgment into His hands.

God cannot be known apart from Jesus. He is the only mediator between man and God. Each and every person's eternal destiny is determined by the acceptance or rejection of the Son of God. He is the "*judge of all the earth*" and He, Jesus is the standard by which we shall be judged.

> For as the Father raiseth up the dead, and quickeneth them; even so the Son quickeneth whom he will. For the Father judgeth no man, but hath committed all judgment unto the Son: That all men should honour the Son, even as they honour the Father. He that honoureth not the Son honoureth not the Father which hath sent him. Verily, verily, I say unto you, He that heareth my word, and believeth on him that sent me, hath everlasting life, and shall not come into condemnation; but is passed from death unto life. Verily, verily, I say unto you, The hour is coming, and now is, when the dead shall hear the voice of the Son of God: and they that hear shall live. For as the Father hath life in himself; so hath he given to the Son to have life in himself; And hath given him authority to execute judgment also, because he is the Son of man. (John 5:21-17)

The Son quickens whoever He wants. Jesus is the author of the new birth; He gives new life, a share for all who believe in eternal life. The Son of God is the judge, whom He justifies is justified indeed, whom He condemns is condemned forever.

This judge first gave His life as the substitute for sinners, to satisfy the divine claims of justice.

All men are already condemned. The divine sentence has already been passed. "The soul that sinned shall surely die." Holiness and justice must be satisfied in God's moral universe.

> The LORD is in his holy temple, the LORD's throne is in heaven: his eyes behold, his eyelids try, the children of men. The LORD trieth the righteous: but the wicked and him that loveth violence his soul hateth. Upon the wicked he shall rain snares, fire and brimstone, and an horrible tempest: this shall be the portion of their cup. For the righteous LORD loveth righteousness; his countenance doth behold the upright. (Psalm 11)

Every day between now and that final condemnation is a gift of grace. Estranged from God, men and women pass their brief time on this earth, dead to what they were created for, insensitive to their Creator, distracting themselves with vanity, dying even while they live, and hurtling towards a final judgment.

> Verily, verily, I say unto you, The hour is coming, and now is, when the dead shall hear the voice of the Son of God: and they that hear shall live.

Into our living death, comes the voice of Jesus, calling us out of the tombs of our own sin, unrighteousness, God rejection and even hatred.

I heard His voice when I was 19 years old. Not physically, but morally and certainly. I had read the Sermon on the Mount, and instantly knew that what I was reading was truth.

Jesus' teaching on the spirituality of the Law of God gripped me. I had thought it enough not to do the act, but when Jesus taught that the demands of the law apply to our inward desires as well as our deeds, I then knew I was a deep sinner.

I was gripped by the conviction of my sin, for about three months. I had never gone to any but our local Catholic church, but I began attending an evangelical, Pentecostal church in the college town where I had been living.

All was alien to my experience of religion. There were no candles, robes or liturgy; the trappings of religion were absent. But the people lifted their hands and sang and wept and literally cried out to One who was obviously on the receiving end of those heartfelt prayers.

Every time they held an altar call at the end of those services, I rushed forward, to try to loose myself from the conviction that I had broken the law of God and was going to go to hell.

But to no avail, for I had no faith, no reason to believe that I could be saved.

Finally after about three months of this I was depressed and in despair. I knew that I was a sinner, so far from God and so hopeless to live the right kind of life.

One day in the depths of my deep sorrow, I realized I was reading the same sentence of the Bible, and not even comprehending one syllable of what I was reading. In my distraction I had just been looping the same verse over and over again.

It was then that a clear thought penetrated my gloomy frame of mind–*look at what you are reading and understand*–the text was 2 Corinthians 5:21–

> For he hath made him to be sin for us, who knew no sin; that we might be made the righteousness of God in him.

I can't explain it other than to say with Jesus, I HEARD the voice of the Son of God. For I *saw it*, instantly. God had made Jesus to become sin for me. He became my substitute on the cross. He took my place in judgment, that we who are sinners and fully know sin, might be "made" (by God, not ourselves) the righteousness of God.

It was then that saving faith came into my heart. I then "*believed on the Son of God*", and entered into everlasting life.

> He that believes on the Son has everlasting life...He that hath the Son hath the life . . . Jesus said, I am the way, the truth and the life.

But what of those who refuse to believe? The only other way is to stay where they are, under the wrath of God that Jesus died to shield us from. Rather than being born again, multitudes would rather remain estranged from God, and (unwittingly) under the very wrath Jesus came to save us from.

> He that believeth not the Son shall not see life; but the wrath of God abideth on him.

How dreadful! That one could come alive to God, be forgiven of their sins, and be guaranteed an entrance into the coming Kingdom of God . . . but should opt instead to remain right where they are, condemned, doomed, alienated from God, and from meaning.

To choose to continue on as the object of God's anger and holy hatred of sin and all that is false. Why? Pride? Rebellion? Will you be damned by your refusal to admit that you are wrong?

Appendix One

The Meaning of Repentance

> There were present at that season some that told him of the Galilaeans, whose blood Pilate had mingled with their sacrifices. And Jesus answering said unto them, Suppose ye that these Galilaeans were sinners above all the Galilaeans, because they suffered such things? I tell you, Nay: but, except ye repent, ye shall all likewise perish. Or those eighteen, upon whom the tower in Siloam fell, and slew them, think ye that they were sinners above all men that dwelt in Jerusalem? I tell you, Nay: but, except ye repent, ye shall all likewise perish. (Luke 13:1-5)

The greatest spiritual breakthroughs I have had, over the 30 some years I have been a Christian, have often come as a result of an insight into the meaning of a simple word or concept.

Words such as *righteousness*, *faith* or *holy*, or concepts such as *purity of heart*, *the blood of Jesus* or *spiritual warfare*, permeated the songs, prayers, scriptures and sermons of the Christianity which I plunged into in the late 1970s.

As I suppose many others have done also, I incorporated those very words and concepts into my own spiritual life, assigning whatever definitions to them that I already had, either by my own past, or by gut instinct. I didn't do this consciously of course.

As I continued at the feet of Jesus, soaking up the Christian teaching through pastors and teachers of the only true faith, it has been when someone opens up a simple but adequate definition of these terms and concepts that my spiritual life has abounded.

I hope in this appendix I can communicate the same kind of breakthrough for someone, as I examine one of those words. I speak of the word *repentance*.

The gospel begins with this word, for in Mark, (the earliest gospel), both Jesus and John the Baptist commence their work, by preaching *repentance* to Israel.

> John did baptize in the wilderness, and preach the baptism of *repentance* for the remission of sins . . . Now after that John was put in prison, Jesus came into Galilee, preaching the gospel of the kingdom of God, And saying, The time is fulfilled, and the kingdom of God is at hand: *repent ye*, and believe the gospel. (Mark 1:4,14-15)

As a former Catholic I must confess that my understanding of the term was muddled, for I confused it at first with "Penance", which is the (false) system of personal recompense for acts of sin committed, usually assigned by the Priest after confession. Penance is an act of abasement or self-mortification to show sorrow for sin.

As a newly saved Christian, I knew that I no longer

needed confession or a Priest to pronounce my absolution. But when I saw Jesus and John call all men to "repent" I still confused the thought with attempts to "make up" for sins I had done, or at least it meant to show that I am sufficiently sorry for them.

Furthermore I didn't know, that I was ignorant of the true meaning of repentance.

I just assumed that it was something about being sorry. I am afraid there are many in church who when they hear the word "repentance" in a sermon or a prayer, the word is just as murkily vague. They know it is negative for sure, and has something to do with feeling bad or sorry, but that's about it. But as a result of several gracious factors; good books, personal Bible study, and hearing good sermons, the vagueness around the word has cleared up.

First of all repentance means to change your mind. The Greek word is *metanoia*, and it means to change your mind.

What was John the Baptist doing as he stood before Israel and called upon them to repent? What is it that we are trying to get people in our generation to do, when we go forth to witness to them?

What was it that Jesus sought to get people to do through His preaching, when He warned, "*Unless you repent you will perish*"?

Everybody on earth has worked out consciously or unconsciously, a "plan of salvation". The problem is that most of those are wrong!

Mine was that one day my good deeds would out

weigh my bad, and I would "get into purgatory", and eventually heaven. I didn't think I knew anyone bad enough to go straight to hell, (maybe Hitler?), or good enough to go to heaven (Mother Teresa?). Most people I knew were in the middle, headed for purgatory.

I am so very glad that I didn't die clinging to that false hope, for I surely would have died in my sins, and perished forever, from the presence of the Lord and the glory of His power, in the lake of fire.

God got through to me and gave me metanoia, i.e., a change of mind. The answer is the same for all, we are trying to get people to change their mind, so that they won't "perish", i.e. be ruined forever!

Why do people need to change their minds?

Because unless people let go of false assumptions about salvation, they will not be able to receive the Salvation of God.

For example, John Baptist was dealing with an error that Israel was clinging to that was "inoculating" them against the Word of God's coming judgment. They thought that because they were children of Abraham (in the flesh), they were immune to any Judgment at all.

> . . . O generation of vipers, who hath warned you to flee from the wrath to come? Bring forth therefore fruits worthy of repentance, and *begin not to say within yourselves, We have Abraham to our father*: for I say unto you, That God is able of these stones to raise up children unto Abraham. And now also the axe is laid unto the root of the trees: every tree therefore which bringeth not forth good fruit is hewn down, and cast into the fire. (Luke 3:7b-9)

Judgment upon Israel was looming, in the days of John the Baptist and of Jesus, but the people were captivated by a "vain imagination", that mere physical descent from Abraham was enough to save them.

They didn't believe they needed God anymore than they already "had" him, as children of Israel. They thought they were saved, just by virtue of being Israel.

But in practice Israel was a God-rejecting "brood of vipers".

(There are many in America, just like them. Christian in name, steeped in the church, but with no real inward affinity with Jesus or the things of God!)

John's task was to get them to see that it is spiritual affinity with Abraham that counts.

Spiritually, were they anything at all like Abraham? Had they left the world as he did? Were they pilgrims, clinging to the promise of worldwide redemption through the "seed of Abraham", the Messiah? Were they looking for a heavenly country or an earthly one?

John also warned them not to be dismayed, that among the stones (Gentiles, dead to God) God would raise up other true children of Abraham. John's preaching was an attempt to get them to "change their minds" about themselves, and their very status before God.

Jesus also preached repentance.

When the rich young ruler asked Jesus, "*Good master, what must I do to inherit eternal life?*", Jesus didn't really answer the question. Instead He asked him a question about the meaning of the word *good.*

> Why do you call me good, there is none good but God . . . ?"

In order to be saved, people need to be made to think. Salvation is about thinking deeply. It is preceded by a "change of mind" that is akin to a paradigm shift.

Jesus knew that it would do no good to share some kind of a "plan of salvation" with the young man, because unless he changed his mind about the meaning of the word *good*, he would never be saved! As long as he was sure that he was "good" and equally sure that as two "good" men, he and Jesus could discuss salvation, this young man was lost. "*There is none good but God* . . ." Repentance is many more things, which we will go into, but first of all, it is simply metanoia, a change of mind.

> **But what think ye?** A certain man had two sons; and he came to the first, and said, Son, go work to day in my vineyard. He answered and said, I will not: but afterward he repented, and went. And he came to the second, and said likewise. And he answered and said, I go, sir: and went not. Whether of them twain did the will of his father? They say unto him, The first. Jesus saith unto them, Verily I say unto you, That the publicans and the harlots go into the kingdom of God before you. For John came unto you in the way of righteousness, and ye believed him not: but the publicans and the harlots believed him: and ye, when ye had seen it, repented not afterward, that ye might believe him. (Matthew 21:28-32)

Notice that Jesus calls us all to think, as His introduction to this parable about repentance. This is because repentance, faith and salvation come to us, only as a consequence of being made to think. As we stated in part 1 of this subject, *repentance* is *metanoia, a change of mind*, about God, His Word, ourselves, salvation, judgment, and eternity.

The very word *repent* is a compound word. *Re* means *again*, and *pent* means *to think*. Thus, to repent means to think again. What we are calling upon men and women to do in our preaching and evangelism is to go back and think again about the most important and eternal things of life.

Everyone who has ever lived has worked out within themselves some kind of a plan of salvation, i.e., thoughts of the afterlife and eternal destiny. It is part of being human to have some thought about what happens after you die. God has put eternity in our hearts, as Ecclesiastes says. The problem is that most of those thoughts are wrong.

The Atheist tells himself that when he dies, it's over. His body decomposes and the atoms and molecules go into the ground. He has it worked out; he need not worry about the afterlife, that is his "plan of salvation"!

The Hindu believes in re-incarnation. If he doesn't get it right in this life, he has thousands of other opportunities to live a human life, and then to become "nothing", Nirvana!

The Muslim hopes that his capricious God will see his observance and take him into heaven. He isn't quite sure if he will, but at in his own deluded mind he thinks that at least he isn't an idolater, or a misguided Christian, or heaven forbid, a Jew, all of which are certain to be thrown into hell.

The nominal Christian has it worked out, that his baptism, or the fact that he has heard that God is love, or perhaps (like I once hoped) that his good deeds would outweigh his bad, and that on the judgment day the scales will tip in his favor.

My point is that it is only human to wonder about death, the afterlife, and to want to resolve these wonderings to satisfaction, and then go on with our own life.

But in all of the cases above, unless these individuals are challenged and compelled to go back and to "think again" about God, salvation, works, judgment etc., none of the above will ever be saved! Jesus said ". . . *unless you repent,* (think again), *you will perish*".

The young man in the parable told his father, "No, I won't go out in the fields for you Father." But as he went on his way, he allowed himself to think again. He changed his mind and did what his father wanted. This is Jesus' teaching on repentance.

The other brother lied to his father, (and no doubt to himself), and never gave it another thought! Just telling his father, "Yes, I will do it", made him feel good, even *righteous* compared to his rebellious brother. But feeling righteous is no substitute for truly being *right with God.* He needed to "think again" also, but failed to do so.

The moral of the story?

John the Baptist tried to get the people of Israel to re-think their stance before God. But because they were circumcised, and descendants of Abraham, according to the flesh, they took (false) comfort, not realizing that John was right, and that judgment was looming over their heads.

The axe was literally at the root of the tree of Israel . . .

But they were fine, they didn't need to reconsider themselves, they had it all worked out in their thoughts. Jesus ran into the same hardness and warned them (and us) of it, citing the prophet Isaiah,

> Therefore speak I to them in parables: because they seeing see not; and hearing they hear not, neither do they understand. And in them is fulfilled the prophecy of Esaias, which saith, By hearing ye shall hear, and shall not understand; and seeing ye shall see, and shall not perceive: For this people's heart is waxed gross, and their ears are dull of hearing, and their eyes they have closed; lest at any time they should see with their eyes and hear with their ears, and should understand with their heart, and should be converted, and I should heal them. (Matthew 13:13-15)

They see . . . but they don't see, they hear . . . but they don't hear, they understand . . . but not really. This is the condition of the unrepentant. They already think they know. No one can get them to "think again", that is to repent. The constant refusal to reconsider, has a hardening and deadening effect on the soul, eventually.

Listen to the prophetic anguish!

> If only they really would be willing to see, and to hear, and truly allow themselves to receive "understanding",

> **they would then be converted**, and I (the LORD) would heal them.

The gospel came to me with power, and shook me to the very core of my being. It changed me, it upended all of my notions about God, and about Jesus, Mary, Heaven, Hell, Purgatory, the church, the basis for judgment, good works, and eternity.

I thought I already knew about all of that, but as I read the Word of God, I was forced to rethink, i.e. repent. But had I refused to allow myself to so much as rethink, I surely would have perished in my sins and been damned forever!

I so thank God for getting my attention, and turning me aside (like Moses' burning bush) and causing me to have to think again. What will happen to this younger generation, for whom through iPads, Walkmans, and iPods, they can program all of their thinking in advance, put the buds in their ears, and tune every other thought out but the ones already programmed? God help us! Grant repentance to this generation!

Repentance is Turning

> O Israel, return unto the Lord thy God; for thou hast fallen by thine iniquity. Take with you words, and turn to the Lord: say unto him, Take away all iniquity, and receive us graciously: so will we render the calves of our lips. Asshur shall not save us; we will not ride upon horses: neither will we say any more to the work of our hands, Ye are our gods: for in thee the fatherless findeth mercy. I will heal

> their backsliding, I will love them freely: for mine anger is turned away from him. (Hosea 14:1-4)

The Hebrew word *Teshuvah*, is translated as *repentance* in the Old Testament. It is a word that means, "to turn". To repent is to turn towards God, or back to God. To sin is to turn away from God. The constant message of the Hebrew prophets was that Israel must "turn" back to the God who had blessed and called them.

Behold the graciousness of God, in this passage from Hosea, pleading with Israel to turn again towards Himself. He goes so far as to give them the words to say!

As a parent I have done such, with an obstinate child, who by his sin has alienated him or herself from we the parents. Yet we plead with them, to be reconciled, even going so far as to tell them what they need to say to us, that fellowship might be restored! "All you have to do is admit you lied . . . we can forgive! We can handle this together, we can get through everything!" God is such a parent, longing for us to turn to Him.

See how He paints a beautiful picture of the possibilities? How He uses the word of Himself, "*If Israel would but* ***turn*** *to me (the LORD), my anger will be* ***turned*** *away from him . . .*"

Another touching glimpse into this desire of the LORD for us to turn, is this from Jeremiah,

> If thou wilt return, O Israel, saith the Lord, return unto me: and if thou wilt put away thine abominations out of my sight, then shalt thou not remove. And thou shalt swear, The Lord liveth, in truth, in judgment, and in

> righteousness; and the nations shall bless themselves in him, and in him shall they glory. For thus saith the Lord to the men of Judah and Jerusalem, Break up your fallow ground, and sow not among thorns. (Jeremiah 4:1-3)

Again note the holy, loving voice calling Israel, "*Return unto Me*", and the beautiful, hopeful picture of the future that could be for them. *Teshuvah* is not merely turning from sin or idols, it is just as much a concept of turning unto God.

He calls upon them to "*Break up your fallow ground* . . ." What is fallow ground? It is ground that once had been plowed and cultivated, but has since become hardened, and resistant to rain or cultivation. Oh that this depraved generation's hearts would be broken, that the LORD might move them to turning.

Moses predicted the entire history of Israel, until the last days. He told them they would forget the Lord, turn away from Him, to worship "strange gods", and to provoke Him to jealousy. As a consequence, they would suffer alienation, and His indignation as well, ultimately being exiled out of the land, and scattered to the very "ends of the earth".

> And the Lord shall scatter you among the nations, and ye shall be left few in number among the heathen, whither the Lord shall lead you. And there ye shall serve gods, the work of men's hands, wood and stone, which neither see, nor hear, nor eat, nor smell. But if from thence thou shalt seek the Lord thy God, thou shalt find him, if thou seek him with all thy heart and with all thy soul. When thou art in tribulation, and all these things are come upon thee, even

> in the latter days, if thou turn to the Lord thy God, and shalt be obedient unto his voice; (Deuteronomy 4:27-30)

The climax of human history will occur, when in the midst of unprecedented world-wide tribulation, Israel finally turns again to the LORD her God. Jesus will come again as a result of it.

The 80th Psalm, is a prayer to the Shepherd of Israel, in which the sad history of Israel's planting, exile and suffering at the hand of Gentiles is recounted. The constant refrain is a prayer that God would "*Turn us again, make thy face to shine upon us, and then we shall be saved!*"

The New Testament also picks up this theme of "turning". For example Paul commends the Thessalonians:

> For they themselves shew of us what manner of entering in we had unto you, and how ye turned to God from idols to serve the living and true God; And to wait for his Son from heaven, whom he raised from the dead, even Jesus, which delivered us from the wrath to come. (1 Thessalonians 1:9-10)

They turned to God from their idols, their expectation changed, they were no longer merely living for today, they longed for the parousia of Jesus.

Finally James teaches *Teshuvah*, when he gives the brilliant and hopeful promise from God–

> Humble yourself under the mighty hand of God and HE will lift you up. Draw near to God and HE will draw near to you . . .

Repentance is nothing unless it is a turning away from that which is sin or evil, or vain, coupled with a turning of the soul and affections to God Himself.

Appendix Two

Repentance is Hating Evil and Loving Good

> For thou, Lord, art high above all the earth: thou art exalted far above all gods. **Ye that love the Lord, hate evil**: he preserveth the souls of his saints; he delivereth them out of the hand of the wicked. (Psalm 97:9-10)

We have been striving to attain the simplest and clearest definition of repentance as possible. We have examined the mental aspects of it, for repentance is first of all a matter of "rethinking" the important things, that people are prone to rationalize, such as God, the soul, heaven, hell and judgment, and the plan of salvation.

Everyone has thoughts about these things, to varying degrees of intensity. As humans, with finite lives but with "eternity in our hearts", we can't avoid such thoughts. There are a large variety of "answers" given to the questions these thoughts raise, the problem is that most of the time these "answers" are wrong.

When God grants repentance to a person, he is made to "rethink" the issues of life, death, God, what it takes to be made right with Him, and the afterlife,

The gospel flies in the face of such false answers as "my good deeds will outweigh my bad", or "purgatory", and brings us to choose truth or error. This is repentance, *metanoia*, "a change of mind".

Furthermore repentance is *Teshuvah*, "turning" from that which was killing us, sin, the world, the supremacy of SELF, The truly repentant is in a constant process of turning away from these idols. But we aren't simply turning away, but ever in the process of turning to . . . God Himself.

> All we like sheep have gone away, we have turned, everyone to His own way . . . (Isaiah 53)

> For ye were as sheep going astray; but are now returned unto the Shepherd and Bishop of your souls. (1 Peter 2:25)

Repentance affects the emotions and deepest affections as well, for the one who is granted repentance from God, now hates the sin that bound and destroyed him, and loves God and His law. God gives us a holy hatred for sin, and by that hatred, we continuously turn away from it.

Repentance involves a revelation from God of the very hatefulness of sin. May God show us all, especially the vacillating Christians, that sin is the evil of evils! It is worse than suffering for it is the very cause of suffering and death. It would actually be better to suffer than to sin.

It is impossible to love God without hating that which God utterly hates. We are to pray that we see sin as God sees it, for repentance engages the affections as well as the mind. Thus the Psalmist exhorts us, **Ye that love the Lord, hate evil.** We must hate the evil of our own indwelling sin, and hate the evil ripening in our own generation, which is deceiving and damning many to hell.

But the humanistic "love" preached for the last generation in the Pentecostal and Evangelical churches has confused many if us on this issue. I am afraid that though there is some truth in the saying, "Love the sinner, hate the sin", there is as much error in it. It isn't always easy to separate the sin from the sinner, and certainly God doesn't.

For example, what are we to make of sinners, who love their own sin, and want to parade it into our churches, demanding tolerance and "unconditional" love? This is the confusion that has led to serious compromise with homosexuality, and Islam.

If God grants us the repentance that utterly abhors sin, and refuses to accept the flaunting of it, or to make peace with it in any fashion, either in ourselves or in our churches, perhaps we can help this drowning generation.

There is a pseudo sophistication, which has seduced many of our leaders into a more "mature" and accepting posture towards unrepentant sinners. These false teachers eschew the doctrine of the Wrath of God and of "propitiation", as though wrath and the demand for a substitution are beneath their concept of a loving God.

They don't believe in the wrath of an infinitely

Holy God anymore, therefore they cannot fear God or hate evil. Furthermore their concept of love is so "tolerant"and accepting, they are actually inviting open homosexuals to come into their assemblies to "worship", and they are actually "apologizing" to them for the "intolerance" of their Christian brothers, who have (rightly) condemned Sodomy in the name of God!

These are the ones who have been teaching in Christian universities, influencing our young Christians, and have infiltrated many pulpits, deceiving, and being deceived. Thus God's people are in danger. They don't have the faith anymore, to resist evil where it should be resisted most– in our churches. They are unsure of what to do.

One would have to believe in a God who utterly and completely hates true evil, and one who had to sacrifice His own Son to satisfy His Holy Justice, in order to resist that magnitude of the iniquity which is being revealed today.

These modern evangelicals are losing their concept of hell and judgment as well, for the same reason– the preaching of "fake love", and the de-emphasis of the wrath of God and His holy hatred for sin. This doesn't bode well, for the church's only real power is the power of truth. We are witnesses of truth. That is our "salt" but what good are we if we lose our savor?

In the two examples I cited, God utterly hates and detests the sin of Sodomy. He calls it detestable, (Leviticus 18:22) unclean, inconvenient, and hateful!

As for Islam, how could this demonic creation possibly "partner" with the church, the only "pillar and ground of the truth" when everything about Islam is lies and murder? All of the gods of the nations are demons! (Psalm 96:5)

We have to beg the Lord for holy repentance, a change of mind, a rethink, a change of heart that causes us to love the things God loves and hate the things God hates! I close with the words of the apostle Jude, as an antidote to the confusion about Love/Hate in the evangelical church:

> These are spots in your love feasts, while they feast with you without fear, serving only themselves. They are clouds without water, carried about by the winds; late autumn trees without fruit, twice dead, pulled up by the roots; raging waves of the sea, foaming up their own shame; wandering stars for whom is reserved the blackness of darkness forever. Now Enoch, the seventh from Adam, prophesied about these men also, saying, "Behold, the Lord comes with ten thousands of His saints, to execute judgment on all, to convict all who are ungodly among them of all their ungodly deeds which they have committed in an ungodly way, and of all the harsh things which ungodly sinners have spoken against Him."
>
> These are grumblers, complainers, walking according to their own lusts; and they mouth great swelling words, flattering people to gain advantage. But you, beloved, remember the words which were spoken before by the apostles of our Lord Jesus Christ: how they told you that there would be mockers in the last time who would walk according to their own ungodly lusts. These are sensual persons, who cause divisions, not having the Spirit. But

you, beloved, building yourselves up on your most holy faith, praying in the Holy Spirit, keep yourselves in the love of God, looking for the mercy of our Lord Jesus Christ unto eternal life And on some have compassion, making a distinction; but others save with fear, pulling them out of the fire, hating even the garment defiled by the flesh. (Jude 12-22)

Appendix Three

Repentance is a Gift of God

> And the servant of the Lord must not strive; but be gentle unto all men, apt to teach, patient, In meekness instructing those that oppose themselves; **if God peradventure will give them repentance to the acknowledging of the truth**; And that they may recover themselves out of the snare of the devil, who are taken captive by him at his will. (1 Timothy 2:24-26)

> When they heard these things, they held their peace, and glorified God, saying, Then hath **God also to the Gentiles granted repentance unto life**. (Acts 11:18)

The Christian journey always begins with repentance. There will be no salvation, no forgiveness, no knowledge of God, and no going to heaven for those who do not repent. Jesus said "*unless you repent, you will perish*".

But what is repentance? We have seen that it is rethinking, changing our mind about what we once thought we knew about God, ourselves, our moral and spiritual condition, heaven, hell, judgment, the spiritual reality, and about Jesus. We have also seen that repentance is *Teshuvah*, the Hebrew word for repentance which means *turning*. To repent is to turn away from idols, or from folly and sin, and unto God Himself, on His terms.

Repentance has a profound effect on the affections as well, for when a person truly repents, He now loves the things of God, and hates the sins which once bound and destroyed him.

> Love not the world, nor the things of the World, for if any one loves the world he has not the love of the Father . . . (1 John 2:15)

There are many examples of this in the Bible, such as the prodigal son "rethinking" about his father, Nebuchadnezzar "changing his mind" about his greatness and sovereignty, Moses realizing that he stood with the slaves, and not with the Egyptians, and Saul of Tarsus, falling in love with Jesus and the Christians, who he once hated and persecuted.

All of these were brought to repentance, they turned away from who they once were, and fully turned towards God, through Jesus.

My point in this article is that repentance isn't something that anyone can "work up at will", rather it is a gift from God. People who are trapped in a wrong way of thinking; in sinful habits and desires, shameful lusts, can't rouse themselves out of these things without God's gracious intervention. God grants unto those who He saves, the gift of repentance.

In my own case, as I was sinking deep in sin in my late teenaged years, I came across a Bible, a gift someone had given my brother. It really was a paraphrase of scripture, called "The Way". One evening I returned from drunken carousing, and saw the Bible on the dresser in our room. A thought occurred to me, "I have never really read the Bible, how could I consider my self truly literate"?

So I began to read the Sermon on the Mount, which I found beautiful, but soon found troubling and convicting. Jesus' interpretation of the spirituality of the law hit me very hard. I thought it would be good enough not to kill a person, or not to commit an act of adultery.

But Jesus' words changed my mind (albeit reluctantly). He was working on my soul, changing my mind about the nature of true righteousness. I was being given a gift, repentance. Now I saw that I had already broken all of the laws of God, and that my inner man was sick, "corrupt according to deceitful lusts", and that I was liable to divine judgment.

My repentance began by turning me away from myself righteousness and sin.

My repentance was completed when I was shown who to turn to. I was in despair one night, because I knew I was damned, and lost, but didn't know how to be saved. I had answered so many "altar calls" trying to shake the guilt, but still had no faith to be saved. I couldn't see how God could forgive my breaking of His law.

Reading the Bible, but so depressed and despairing

that I really didn't even know what it was I was reading, I had a clear thought penetrate my mind, "Look at what you are reading and understand it!" I had been so distracted by sorrow and fear of judgment, I had been reading the same verse over and over again and couldn't even tell you what it was!

I looked again at the scripture,

> He made Him who knew no sin, to be sin for us, that we might be made the righteousness of God in Him. (2 Corinthians 5:21)

Suddenly I perceived why Jesus died on the cross; He was taking my place in judgment and bearing my sin, that I might be accepted before God as He was. Jesus became "me" so that I could become "Him" as far as status before God!

God uses scripture, and people, and even circumstances to get a person to "turn aside and look at the burning bush", or to "ponder the path" of their feet, and "consider their own end". But in the final analysis, it is not going to happen unless the Holy Spirit of God gives a person the gift of repentance.

I now realize that what happened to me in the years 1977-1978 was the fulfillment of the words of Jesus,

> And when he (The Holy Spirit)is come, he will reprove the world of sin, and of righteousness, and of judgment: Of sin, because they believe not on me; Of righteousness, because I go to my Father, and ye see me no more; Of judgment, because the prince of this world is judged. (John 16:8-10)

We must pray that God will grant repentance to this generation, for without it, they perish forever. The minds of many have been so blinded by secular humanism, atheism, Islam, humanistic "christianity" . . . anything but the Truth. But God is not willing that any should perish, but that all will come to repentance. He is dealing with people by His Spirit, urging them to get right with Him, calling them to Himself.

Other Books by Pastor Bill Randles

Making War in the Heavenlies: A different look at Spiritual Warfare"- (1994) Pastor Bill was asked in 1994 to explain why he wasn't leading his church into various aspects of city wide spiritual warfare exercising, such as prayer walking, March for Jesus, naming the demons over the city, binding and loosing ,etc. Out of that explanation came this book, which discusses not only the heretical practices listed above, bit the true biblical teaching on spiritual warfare.

Weighed and Found Wanting: Putting the Toronto Blessing in Context- (1995)- Thousands of Christians were traveling to the Toronto Airport Vineyard to experience "a new anointing", and Spiritual Drunkeness. Was this really "as a rushing mighty wind from heaven" as its proponents claimed? Pastor Bill refutes this notion, having traced the "revival" back to its roots in the Manifested Sons of God heresy, once rebuked and rejected by the Assemblies of God, but now widely accepted as a mighty revival.

Beware the New Prophets (1997) - In this book Pastor Bill explains the origins and theology of the "prophetic movement" which emerged out of the Latter Rain and Manifested Sons of God heresy. This book is valuable because Pastor also shows the biblical tests of true and false prophecy.

Mending The Nets: Themes and Commentary of First John - In this book Pastor Bill explores the undergirding themes of first John, such as eternal life, the tests of eternal life, true and false faith, the Gnostic redefinition of the knowledge of God, and the true knowledge of God. Like John, Pastor Bill takes us back to the beginning, the first thing revealed in the gospel of Jesus . This commentary is relevant to the current apostasy in the church.

A Sword On The Land: The Muslim World in Bible Prophecy - (2013) The 2011 "Arab Spring" was significant, but not for the reasons the world hoped for. Pastor Bill, in a very readable style, explains that rather than being a movement towards democracy in the Arab world, the real significance was the setting in place of the nations of the Middle East for the fulfillment of endgames prophecies.

CPSIA information can be obtained
at www.ICGtesting.com
Printed in the USA
FFOW01n0718151115
18525FF